EVERY DAY WAS SUMMER

Every Day was Summer

Childhood memories of Edwardian
days in a small Welsh town

Oliver Wynne Hughes

Illustrations by the author and by
Andrew and Sara Hughes

GOMER PRESS
1989

First impression—1989
Second impression—1991

© Oliver Wynne Hughes

ISBN 0 86383 516 3 (Hardback)

ISBN 0 86383 532 5 (Softback)

Printed by J. D. Lewis and Sons Ltd., Gomer Press, Llandysul, Dyfed.

This book is dedicated to Laura,
Elsie and Beatrice, three young
girls who grew up in a golden age.

CONTENTS

Foreword ix

Preface xi

Introduction xv

Chapter 1: Mother and Father 1

Chapter 2: Childhood Games and Customs 12

Chapter 3: Schooldays 22

Chapter 4: The Shops 29

Chapter 5: The Beach 38

Chapter 6: Golf 43

Chapter 7: Church and Chapel 52

Chapter 8: The English in Harlech 63

Chapter 9: Life in Service 96

Chapter 10: Farm Life 103

Chapter 11: Cwm Bychan 114

Chapter 12: Wartime 117

Epilogue: Men of Harlech 124

FOREWORD

I have been asked by the author, a valued friend, to write a short fore-word to this book. While honoured to be asked, I was concerned about what I could say that would enhance an already charming collection of memories of Harlech in the early part of the twentieth century that many people hold dear to this day.

I use the word concern deliberately, because I know that had I been the 13th Earl of Winchilsea, living in Harlech at the time, my own social, political and moral beliefs would have prevented me from assuming the role of local benefactor and distributing occasional largesse to the inhabitants. I am aware that times, customs, values, and codes of conduct are all subject to change, in my view, quite rightly, and holding Liberal values today is something quite different from the Liberal values current in 1910. I suppose this is easy to say with hindsight, 80 years on, but I think it has to be said.

By making this statement I do not wish to diminish in any way the happy memories that come through so vividly in this book. I found it fascinating and illuminating, as it provides us with a glimpse of life in a small and remote Welsh town where so much was changing.

The author has done something for us all by collecting together people's memories and reminiscences as well as putting them all in context. All too often personal history is forever lost because no one records it. Happily, this has not happened in this case because one individual has taken the time, and the special care, to preserve it.

It is perhaps fitting that I, too, possess a treasured memory of Harlech, in the company of the author, his family and mine, spending a delightful, sunny, 'summer day' together in that lovely old town.

May, 1989   *The Earl of Winchilsea & Nottingham*

PREFACE

This is first of all the story of three sisters who lived in a small Welsh town, Harlech, in the years before 1914.

Laura, born 1896, Elsie, born 1902 and Beatrice, born 1905, together with their brother Jack who was some years older, grew up in this lovely old town in those golden Edwardian years when every day seemed like summer, before everything was swept away in the holocaust of the First World War.

The stories of childhood told by Laura, my mother and Elsie and Beatrice, my aunts, have fascinated me for nearly forty years and now at last I have put their memories and keepsakes on record, to tell a story that tries to do some justice to three young lives before their recollections are lost for ever. Their brother Jack died in 1952, in Harlech and, sadly, Laura too has now gone, dying in 1979 at the age of eighty-two. Elsie and Beatrice, however, both in their eighties, are fit and well, Elsie still living in North Wales and Beatrice in Malta.

Almost inevitably, as I visited Harlech over the years, I met others who had stories and anecdotes to contribute. Their memories, too, have gradually become woven into this mini-history of early twentieth century Harlech, and are little jewels in themselves. In this connection I am particularly indebted to three First World War veterans, two still living locally, for the time they have given me in telling their story—William Evans, Johnny Williams and Griff Thomas. I have sat for hours and listened as they talked, for their memories are still crystal clear. To others, relatives of those who died in that grim war, I am grateful for their kindness in letting me borrow treasured photographs and letters—Jenny Humphreys, Annie Wyndham Thomas who, sadly died recently, and Olwen Williams, all of whom lost brothers in the war, and Mary Pugh, also sadly deceased, who shared with me her sweet memories of a husband who died some years after the war of wounds sustained at Gaza.

It is perhaps fitting that I devote these memories of the First World War to the last chapter of the book, and that this should be entitled 'Men of Harlech'. It is my own tribute to those who fought, those who returned as well as those who died, and who are all, in some way, casualties of that most terrible of wars.

I am grateful also to the Earl of Winchilsea and Nottingham who has shown such interest and who has so kindly agreed to write the Foreword, and to Sir Osmond Williams who has lent me exquisite photographs of his family and of his own father who was himself killed in the very first action of the Welsh Guards in September 1915.

I greatly appreciate the helpful comments and information given to me by Dr. Lewis Lloyd of Coleg Harlech and by Mr. Martin Eckley, Librarian of the College. I am grateful to Mr. David Figg of Kodak for information about Mr. George Davison, to Mr. Harry Fairbrother, former Secretary of the Royal St. David's Golf Club, for access to papers on the history of the Club, to Mr. Dudley Balch, Mrs. Pamela Proctor and Mr. Dudley Maidment who kindly lent me valuable personal documents and photographs, and Mrs. Kathy Henderson of the Rudolf Steiner School at Tremadog for permission to visit and photograph Tan-yr-Allt.

I am indebted to Miss Bessie Owen for stories about her father, to Mrs. Beryl Thomas for her memories of the Graves household, to the Rev. Peter James for information about St. Tanwg's Church, to Mr. and Mrs. Neville Brown of Plas Cafe and to others who have been so helpful in various ways—Mrs. Gwenda Jones, Mrs. Mary Esau, Mr. Michael Baki, Mr. Elwyn Griffiths, Mrs. Peggy Thomas, Mr. James Nelson and to Mrs. Marian Jones who was so patient with my rusty Welsh!

I am grateful to my sister Phyllis who did so much to encourage my dear mother to tell her stories during her terminal illness, to my wife Kim who has helped and encouraged me in so many ways, and my daughter Caroline who translated my writing on to an old typewriter, although the brunt of the typing has been borne by Miss Andrea Wallen and Mrs. Diana Owen.

Finally, I am proud to acknowledge the help given to me by the Commonwealth War Graves Commission, by the Regimental Head-quarters Welsh Guards, by the Museum of the Royal Welch Fusiliers at Caernarfon, by the Museum of the King's Royal Rifle Corps at Winchester, by the Royal Navy Museum, by the House of Commons Library, by the Gwynedd County Council Archive Department,

Debretts Peerage, the *Daily Telegraph*, Tonbridge School, the Dickens Museum, Liverpool University Archives, the City of Manchester Art Gallery and the staff of the library at Blaenau Ffestiniog.

September, 1989   Oliver Wynne Hughes

INTRODUCTION

Those who visit Harlech for the first time, and who have heard something of it in history and song, must find it surprisingly small. It is, indeed, small, with a population of little more than a thousand souls. The 1981 Census showed that the population of Llandanwg parish, which includes Harlech, was 1,525. You could walk around the whole town in half a morning, in less time perhaps than it would take you to walk the castle ramparts. Yet it would be foolish to pass through it too quickly for it is a place full of character and, as our history books remind us, with a fascinating story to tell.

Some believe that the name 'Harlech' is derived from the Welsh *hardd lech* (beautiful slate, or stone); others claim that it is more simply *ar lech* (*on* slate or stone). Certainly no-one can question the rocky nature of the terrain, lying as it does on the outer rim of the mountain fastness of Snowdonia. It is no wonder that Edward I

Harlech Castle.

Dudley Maidment collection

XV

selected this site for one of the royal castles of Wales, part of that ring of fortresses built to subdue the Welsh. It stands on a crag over two hundred feet high, in one of the most magnificent settings of any castle in Britain.

For many years during the middle ages it played its part in the intertwined histories of England and Wales, in the grim wars of those turbulent times. Later it played a crucial role in the no less bloody battles of the Wars of the Roses and in the Civil War. That most stirring tune in any military band repertoire, 'The March of the Men of Harlech', commemorates the heroic resistance of a small Welsh garrison as they resisted siege in the Lancastrian Cause during the Wars of the Roses. In the Civil War, too, it was the last of the king's castles to fall. Now, instead of the sounds of steel upon steel or the thunder of besieging cannon, all we hear are the screech of gulls and the whoops of children echoing war cries long silent, while sheep graze in the grass-covered moat and brightly coloured sailing boats beckon from the bay.

After the Civil War, there followed centuries of relative stagnation. The town's population growth was virtually static and had reached no more than five hundred or so by 1851 and 1,200 by 1901. By the beginning of the new century, however, Harlech had been discovered as a pleasant holiday resort, and it became a favoured watering place of the English aristocracy, perhaps uniquely so in Wales. The Ormsby-Gores, who had lived in Glyn, their Harlech home, for a hundred years or more and who had taken the name of Harlech when the Baronetcy was created in 1876, were now joined by the Earls of Winchilsea and Amherst. The families of those in trade and industry also came—the Frys, the Birds, the Pilkingtons, as well as famous writers and artists—Robert Graves, Siegfried Sassoon, George Bernard Shaw, Augustus John. They all found an area of outstanding natural beauty, a mild and pleasant climate, sheltered from cold east winds by a curtain of hills, and an old town dominated by its magnificent castle.

Edward's stronghold, built between 1283 and 1290, can be seen on the skyline for many miles, with the ground on which it stands falling sharply away. Years ago that rocky outcrop plunged straight down into the foaming waters below, but with the gradual extension of the

Harlech, 1921.

salt marshes there has been created an expanse of land, nearly a mile in width, between castle and sea, on which stand patches of gorse and broom, buttercups, dog roses, mustard, even wild orchids. Here, on the flat salt marshes, Morfa Harlech, new development has taken place, the Harlech Comprehensive School, council estates and caravan sites, allowing the old town above to remain relatively unchanged.

Between the salt marshes and the sea lie some of the most magnificent sand dunes in Europe, vast mounds forty to fifty feet high, set in wild and wonderful shapes, almost fortresses and castles in themselves. Beyond these in turn is a stretch of flat golden sand, over five miles in length, from which bathers plunge into the waves that sweep into Cardigan Bay.

Behind the town the gentle hills which merge into the Rhinog range are dotted with grey stone farms with captivating names—Cae Du (Black Field), Rhiw Goch (Red Hill), Lasynys-fach (Small Green Island), Rhyd Galed (Hard Ford), while to the north in superb backdrop stand the mountain peaks of Snowdonia.

Across Cardigan Bay lies Cricieth with its own distinctive castle which, with Harlech, form twin protective sentinels for the town of

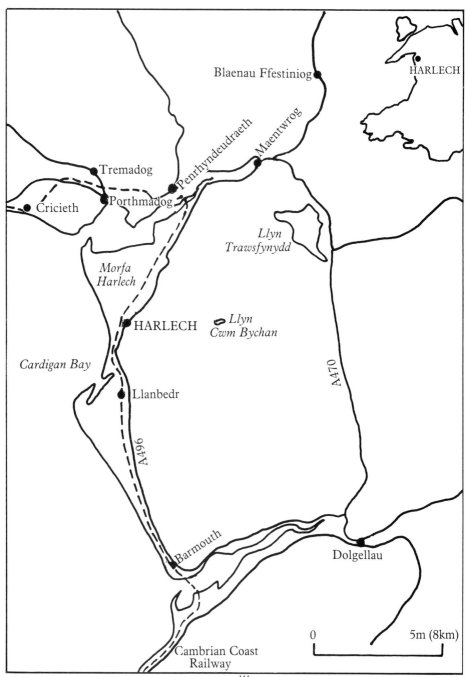

Blaenau Ffestiniog

HARLECH

Maentwrog

Penrhyndeudraeth

Tremadog

Porthmadog

Cricieth

Llyn
Trawsfynydd

Morfa
Harlech

HARLECH

Llyn
Cwm Bychan

Cardigan Bay

A470

Llanbedr

A496

Barmouth

Dolgellau

0   5m (8km)

Cambrian Coast
Railway

Porthmadog. This little port was famous in the latter half of the nine-teenth century for shipping the famous Blaenau Ffestiniog grey-blue slate, carried on the twelve-mile journey by the Ffestiniog Railway, built for that purpose but now more celebrated perhaps as a tourist attraction. Blaenau slates roofed many nineteenth century British towns and cities, part of Buckingham Palace and the government offices of Whitehall. They were used in the rebuilding of Hamburg after the disastrous fire of 1842 and they capped the municipal build-ings of Sydney during the rapid expansion of that city in the last years of the century.

In the days before the First World War it was the slate caverns of Blaenau Ffestiniog that provided the bulk of employment in this area of North Wales. At its height, in the 1890s, the slate industry employed more than 6,000 men in thirteen quarries, the biggest being the Oakley, Maenofferen, Llechwedd and, to a lesser extent, Voty. In those days Blaenau was a lively and flourishing town of some 13,000 people but, sadly, the Great War stopped the export of slate to Germany, then the biggest overseas market. Production was slashed and the population declined, although there are now hopeful signs of a revival, with an increasing tourist trade and a renewed international interest in slate as a roofing material.

As Blaenau declined so, too, did Porthmadog, not just as a seaport but as a home of Welsh shipbuilding, for fine sailing ships had been built there for many years. The Western Ocean Yachts, as they were called, possessed a grace and beauty rarely equalled in the history of sail, and have been described as the finest all-round small merchant sailing ships ever built in Britain. They were fast and efficient, and they were admired wherever they went throughout the world. But with the demise of the stately windjammer there declined also that other employment that had attracted so many of the young men of the area—seafaring, traditionally a favoured profession in this part of Wales. Unlike the Scots or the Irish, life in the army had rarely attracted the Welsh, especially as the chapels, and Lloyd George and the Welsh Liberal Party too, prior to the First World War, held that soldiering was sinful. Despite the fact that Welsh bowmen played a stirring and crucial role in royal victories at Crecy, Poitiers and Agincourt, despite the fact that Welshmen fought at Rorke's Drift, in the battles of the First and Second World Wars, and in the Falklands too, the Welsh cannot really be described as a military people. Consequently, Wales has produced few men of great military stature. But seafaring was a different matter. One hundred and fifty North Welshmen were in the fleet that sacked Cadiz in 1596 and, later, Welsh sea captains became known as far away as Australia, South America, the Caribbean and the Pacific Coast of the USA. Close connections grew up between this part of Wales and the great seaport of Liverpool, with Welsh sailors graduating from their small ships to take command of the famous Liverpool square-riggers. Even Lloyd George himself wanted to be the master of a sailing ship, and Welsh sailors rivalled the achievements and reputation of their West Country counterparts. Amongst famous Welsh seamen were the illustrious pirate Henry (later Sir Henry) Morgan, Admiral Sir Hugh Evan-Thomas, who commanded the 5th Battle Squadron at Jutland and John Pritchard, for many years Master of that most loved of ships, the old *Mauretania*.

The decline of slate quarrying and shipping, both of which had given so much local employment, was a severe blow to the region and to Harlech, whose menfolk had played no small part in their development. Fortunately there was some compensation in an increase in visitors to the town during the closing years of the nineteenth century, from the rest of Wales and from England. Here there were two main attractions. First, there was the establishment of the Harlech Festival. Founded in 1867, partly out of the Temperance movement, it was held in the grounds of the castle each year in summer. Choirs of up to 1,500 voices sang under the direction of some of Britain's most famous conductors, and people came from all over Britain to listen to these performances. Sadly, however, these festivals coincided so frequently with wet and miserable weather conditions, with consequent financial losses, that they were discontinued in the early 1930s.

Of even more importance in the growth of Harlech as a tourist resort was the founding in 1894 of the St. David's Golf Club (later the Royal St. David's). Here was to be the ultimate attraction that was to make Harlech a mecca for that special tourist in the decade before the First World War, the moneyed Edwardian aristocrat. Those visitors, sadly, have gone forever. But what is apparent now is a resurgence of more general interest. With such a phenomenal growth in post-war tourism, English and Continental visitors come to North Wales in increasing numbers each year, attracted to Harlech and its surroundings by the contrasting beauty of sea and mountain, and many of whom choose to remain and settle in the area.

But Harlech is not just a summer playground; it is also a place of learning and culture, with an important part being played by Coleg Harlech, a residential adult education institution founded in 1927 and which, for more than sixty years, has provided students with opportunities for individual development in a congenial and pleasant environment. Important, too, has been the growth of good hotels and restaurants. In an area once barren of hope of ever finding something to satisfy the inner man, there are now many fine eating places which provide memorable meals in agreeable surroundings.

But, above all else, the lasting impression left on visitors is that breathtaking sweep of beach and bay. When the Queen, then Princess Elizabeth, came to North Wales in 1947, the motorcade stopped just outside the town to give her an opportunity to stand and admire that same view. She stayed there for some time, and the spot is now commemorated by a memorial plaque. It is no bad standpoint from which to take in a panorama that is perhaps unsurpassed anywhere in the British Isles.

CHAPTER 1

Mother and Father

'Mother was left a widow relatively early,' says Elsie, 'at the age of thirty-nine, and brought up four children on her own. Jack was the eldest, then there were us three girls—Laura, myself and Beatrice, the youngest. In those days before the First World War there was no state aid. Life was poor and she worked hard. In some ways she was lucky in that employment could be found with seasonal visitors, for Harlech was a popular holiday place with the English aristocracy. Regular visitors were Lord and Lady Winchilsea and Lord and Lady Amherst, while other famous holidaymakers were the Frys, the Pilkingtons and the Cadburys. Mother worked regularly for the Winchilseas. In the winter, when they were not in residence, she looked after

Mother in 1933, aged 66.

Author's collection

1

the household linen. In the summer she helped in one of their two houses, either in the Plas or at Bron-y-Graig, although the family brought from London a full staff who arrived by train some days before.

'Mother was a strict person and the possessor of a strong character, but she was always fair and straightforward. One of only four English people in Harlech she was well thought of, respected and popular, even though she never learned Welsh. Indeed, throughout all her eighteen years in the town she never managed any of the language at all, although she must have understood more than she let us know.

'Everybody was kind to her, and made special efforts to help the family. Men who worked on the golf course brought her rabbits; indeed at times we seemed to live on rabbits in one form or another, either pie, stewed or roast. In mock resignation she would often quote the following lines:

> Rabbit hot and rabbit cold,
> Rabbit young and rabbit old,
> Rabbit tender and rabbit tough,
> But thank the Lord, we've had enough!

Lord and Lady Winchilsea were also extremely generous in giving food and clothing. Many Harlech families, too, often just as poor as we were, helped whenever they could.

'She was always clean and neat, and we children went to school well-scrubbed. Sunday clothes, many of which she made herself, meant Sunday clothes, and were worn on Sundays and no other day. Our cottage in Pentre'r Efail, rented from a local shopkeeper, Johnny Morris, at 1/6d per week, was small but spotlessly clean and comfortable. There was always a roaring fire and a brightly lit oil lamp. Mother was fond of reading, and as we passed the window on our return from Sunday School on winter evenings she'd be sitting in the rocking chair with a book in her lap, with the fire crackling in front of her and the lamp's warm glow behind. As poor as she was she liked her fire and her light. Most houses only had candles, but she had her lamp. These were her own little luxuries.

'Her daily routine consisted of rising at six o'clock, then working until lunchtime at the Plas. She would return home to prepare our

2

Pentre'r Efail: Laura standing by the wall, holding Beattie; Elsie third from the left, c.1908. Their cottage is the white-faced building on the left.

Author's collection

lunch, though often she would be given something hot to bring with her—stew or hot-pot, sometimes roast lamb. She would make soup and there would be suet pudding and hot syrup, or spotted dick and white sauce. On such days we ate well. After lunch she would return to work, often staying to help with the washing up after the Winchilseas' evening meal. She'd come home utterly exhausted at about nine o'clock, but then she would have to set-to doing her own washing, ironing and cleaning, working sometimes until two or three o'clock in the morning.

'She was a great Royalist and a Conservative through and through. Conservatives in Wales were always identified with Englishness and she herself wore a large blue rosette at election time, even in 1906 when every one of the thirty-four Welsh constituencies elected a Liberal. This public display of Conservative loyalty was unique in Harlech and it was a source of great embarrassment to us. Children at school would shout, *"Hen Dori 'di dy fam"* (Your mother's an old Tory). We used to beg her not to wear that rosette, but she wore it all the more firmly to show her pride and allegiance.

3

'She was a bit of a suffragette too. Mrs. Owen, the butcher's wife, who was also suspected of being one, would give us sealed envelopes and whisper conspiratorially, "Don't open them, they're for your mother." But we did open them, of course, and found political tracts and pamphlets with pictures of Mrs. Pankhurst. In those days the very name of Suffragette was something mysterious, even unpleasant. We'd say, "Here comes a suffragette", and run like blazes!

'For our holidays we would go to Liverpool. We were fortunate that mother had relatives there and our friends in Harlech thought it wonderful that we travelled so far. To them it must have seemed like a journey to the moon, because none of our friends went further than ten miles away, to Barmouth, and that was only for one day in the summer. That was their annual treat. When we came back from Liverpool they could hardly believe the stories we told—about electric tramcars, shops and picture palaces. Their mouths would drop open and at such times we ourselves would feel like aristocrats.

'Mother was a very religious woman and went to church every Sunday. There was only one English service, in the mornings, and she went regularly throughout her time in Harlech. She never went to bed without kneeling and praying for our safety, and when we grew up and went our way in the world she admonished us to keep our faith, as she had done through the years.

'For much of her life mother was lame. In 1911, at the age of forty-four, she fell downstairs at the cottage, only over the last few steps but, with the passageway being so small, she fell awkwardly. It was a Saturday afternoon and I shall always remember it. I was out playing and someone came to tell me that she'd fallen. I recall running wildly homewards, for I was devoted to mother. I was frightened of the wind blowing on her, because if anything happened to her we'd end up as orphans. I suppose it was a clinging sort of love. On that afternoon the house was full of people and she was lying on the sofa in great pain. Old Dr. Richard Jones was there, but he wasn't able to do very much except put on cold compresses. Her ankle was badly swollen and obviously broken, but there was no hospital in Harlech—the nearest was at Bangor, more than forty miles away. The local doctor most proficient in setting broken bones, Dr. Parry, from Penrhyn, was in London and wasn't due back until the next day. By the time he arrived

4

at five p.m. on the Sunday her leg and foot were black. I could hear her screaming and I remember running around in despair. The two doctors were there together. Dr. Parry was a small man but Dr. Jones was huge, with an Edward VII beard, given to wearing large hats and sleeveless coats. He had a deep gruff voice and we used to run miles when we saw him because he frightened us so much. But he was kindness itself, and he would interest himself in us children. If he saw Beattie out playing, perhaps too late in his opinion, he would tell her, in his deep growl, to run off home to bed. He had a special spot in his heart for Beattie because at birth he'd given her only a few months to live, for she was very tiny and weak. But with mother's care she had improved and become a healthy and lovely young girl.

'On this dreadful Sunday it was Dr. Jones's job to hold mother down as Dr. Parry manipulated the leg. But she was a strong woman and, heavy as the doctor was, it was still an effort to control her struggles. She beat at him with clenched fists. "You're doing the job," he said to Dr. Parry, "and I'm getting the beating." But he turned to mother and said, "Carry on Mrs. Williams, thump me as much as you like." Two hours or more went by while they tried to straighten the leg and set it. It was a terrible task, for nearly every bone in her ankle was broken and there was hardly one whole piece they could work on. After much perseverance, however, they succeeded in putting together the horrendous jig-saw.

'It was to be a full year before she could move without crutches. Then she went to Liverpool for convalescence. While there she was sent by Dr. Parry to see Sir Robert Jones, probably the most eminent bone specialist in the world at the time. A gentle and kindly man, he held free surgeries at his famous clinic in Nelson Street for those who couldn't afford to pay. "Well, Mrs. Williams," he said, "I cannot do anything more to your leg. I tell you this much," he continued. "If you'd come to this hospital when you first broke it there is little doubt that we would have amputated. Young Dr. Parry saved your leg. Very clearly he is a most remarkable man."

'For years to come, bone chippings used to work their way out through small holes in her ankle. She resorted to the family remedy, the "ointment", a homemade, foul smelling concoction made from a recipe that she prepared and "cooked" from a mixture of onions, resin

5

and herbs. It was effective for all sorts of ailments in the Harlech household, from sore-throats to backache, from boils to bronchitis. "It had enough drawing power to pull a horse and cart stuck fast in mud," said one local farmer.' (The original recipe apparently came from an elderly relative in Anglesey who had been given a substantial pension for life for curing the chronic cataract of a wealthy local spinster.)

Every night of her life their mother would put the ointment on a clean piece of linen and this would be strapped around her leg. Gradually, over the weeks, a large scab would form over the affected parts, blocking the tiny holes. Eventually, perhaps after two or three months, the children would hear her groaning in the night as the ointment drew out the poisons. The following morning, when she unwrapped the bandage, the scab would be gone, and on the dressing would be dozens of pieces of tiny bone. There would then be freedom from pain for another few months, while the whole process of scab growth would start all over again. Years later, another doctor, elsewhere, expressed his conviction that that simple remedy had saved her leg, otherwise severe gangrene would have set in. So it was a combination of country doctoring and country medicine that performed an almost miraculous cure. As far as Dr. Parry was concerned it became common knowledge that he had received a warm letter of congratulation from the great man himself, Sir Robert Jones. 'And,' says Elsie, 'as far as the ointment is concerned, it still remains in family use.'

'Father died at an early age,' says Laura, 'of tuberculosis. He was a seafarer and was away for two or three years at a time. He often came home penniless because he'd spent his money, on drink in particular. Mother hoped all down the years that, eventually, he would bring money home, but he rarely had any to give her. This was a sad part of our life.

'He had run away from home in Harlech when he was fourteen. There was a younger sister who suffered from consumption, and he adored her. Her name was Laura, too, and I was called after her. One day he came home from school to find that his stepmother had given her a thrashing for some small misdemeanour and had locked her in the washhouse, crying bitterly. In his fury, for he had a violent

Father, with unknown companion.

temper, he got hold of his stepmother and gave her a sound beating. But he knew that when his father came home he would get a good beating in turn so, rather than wait for that, he packed his bags and ran away. He travelled to Liverpool and from there he found a ship and went away to sea.

'Young Laura died shortly after, as much from a broken heart as from her dreadful disease, for she'd loved him as much as he loved her. She had been a beautiful child, as many consumptives were, with a lovely transparent complexion. Her father didn't survive much longer, for he never got over the shock of his son's departure. On his deathbed he said he would give anything to see Jack once more. But they never met again.'

'When father returned from sea he made Liverpool his home,' says Elsie, 'and he didn't go back to Harlech. Eventually he met mother, proposed to her, and was accepted, telling her both before and after their marriage that he had no family, that he was an orphan. However, one Sunday afternoon, they were sitting in their parlour when there came a knock on the door. Mother answered and there stood a middle-aged couple. "Mrs. Williams?" the gentleman asked. She nodded. "I'm Jack's elder brother," he replied. "From Harlech." Mother straight away asked them in, and there, in that Liverpool parlour, Jack and William, brothers who hadn't met for years, embraced. William then explained that someone from Harlech had seen Jack in a dockside tavern and had written home, thus prompting their visit. Uncle William tried hard to persuade him to return to Harlech, offering him work on his farm, for it was clear that father was not in the best of health. But he declined, as he was now due to go back to sea.'

'By then our brother Jack was a young baby and shortly afterwards, in 1896, I was born,' says Laura. 'But father's health had deteriorated further by the next time he came home, and when Uncle William repeated his offer of employment mother and he decided to pack their bags and go. Shortly before they went Elsie was born, in 1902, Beattie being born in Harlech three years later.'

'He worked on uncle's farm for a while,' says Elsie, 'but his health continued to fail. He suffered for three years, but he was a poor patient, not easy to look after, for he wanted alcohol all the time. Apart

8

Father's brother, Uncle 'Cae Du'.

9

The three sisters, 1960. From left to right: Beatrice, Laura and Elsie.

from being nursemaid and doctor mother also had to go out to work to support the family in any way she could, by helping in the big houses and by sewing. They'd been married fifteen years and throughout that time she'd had a terribly hard and difficult life with him. He died in 1906. She was a widow for 45 years until her death in 1951.'

'I remember father's funeral well,' says Laura, 'but although I was sad it was the "impression" of it all that affected me most: Elsie's chestnut hair shining in the weak autumn sun; myself in black with a large hat with a bow at the back; mother in black crepe and veil, silent all the way in the long carriage ride to the cemetery, gazing all the while at the white-flecked sea; the long stretch of walking mourners behind the cortege . . .'

After so many years of illness and a lifetime spent fighting the hardships of life aboard those old sailing ships there was perhaps some consolation for the family that he had died at home and was buried on a sunny October day in Llanfair cemetery just outside Harlech.

11

CHAPTER 2

Childhood Games and Customs

'We had a wonderful childhood,' says Elsie. 'As in all poor communities there was little in the way of formal entertainment. But there are wonderful memories of so much homemade fun.'

A focal point of their play were the rocks of Pen Graig, a stony outcrop a little outside the town, overlooking the lovely Cardigan Bay. Here they would go most days after school. Perhaps the most frequent game was 'Weddings'. Individually chosen rocks and nooks were the houses, the girls dressing up in whatever finery they could beg or borrow from home. The boys, playing the part of husbands, always seemed to be sea captains, with the trees on Pen Graig named after the big ships of those times—*Olympic, Lusitania, Mauretania, Aquitania.* Quite what ships' captains were doing in the 'rigging'—the branches of the trees—was never quite certain, but in the 'rigging' they would be, swinging from branch to branch while the girls waved to them.

Bronwen Terrace and Pen Graig from Harlech Castle.

Gwynedd Archives Services

12

'We would cry at their departure, wring our hands and wave our damp handkerchiefs.' The next thing of course would be the 'returning'. The girls would make a feast of mud pies trimmed with daisies and buttercups. At times they would try to improve on that by gathering blackberries and attempt some sort of pie with lardless flour taken from home, fashioned into a dough and placed on plates of slate. Then, everything prepared, they would rush to the 'quayside' to greet their returning loved ones.

The next most popular game was 'Chapel'. They would sing their hymns in front of a rock outcrop which was the 'pulpit'. Behind this was a larger rock which was the 'organ'. Imitating their elders, they paraded their way to chapel with parasols of fern trimmed with wild flowers—primroses, buttercups or violets. One would take the part of the minister, another would be the organist. Deacons would sit at the front, facing the congregation sitting on tiers of stone. The girls were dressed demurely in simulated Sunday Best, often not even simulated, for skirts and feather boas would be 'borrowed' for the occasion. These clothes were always much more exciting than their own, and more than made up for the inevitable spanking that would follow for, as Elsie recalls, 'Mother would always find out, no matter how carefully I replaced the offending garment.'

It was all taken so seriously. 'I remember on one occasion,' says Elsie, 'a lovely summer evening, the "preacher" and the "deacon", not forgetting the "organist", were leading us all in lusty Welsh singing, the words of every verse, of course, known by heart. When we finished there came the sound of clapping. We turned in dismay to find a group of English visitors listening to us, thinking it all very amusing no doubt. As we stood, somewhat embarrassed, they told us how much they'd enjoyed our singing. Then, to our delight and astonishment, one of the gentlemen gave us half-a-crown, putting it on the slate "collecting-plate". After they'd gone we shared it out between us, a penny or so each I think it was, but to us it was a fortune. We couldn't get to the shops quickly enough. "Chapel" finished early that day!'

Pen Graig was also a paradise for courting couples. 'I remember one day finding a florin in the grass,' says Elsie. 'A little further on was a shilling, and then a few pennies. I whooped with glee with every one I found. It was like a magic dream. I can only conclude that a couple had been so involved in their love-making the night before that he just hadn't noticed his pocket was getting lighter!'

Another favourite game was 'Funerals'. Elsie had a beautiful china doll given to her by one of Lady Winchilsea's maids. She kept it for a long time but eventually it broke. 'I was terribly upset, because I was very fond of dolls, of this one in particular, and I loved to dress them. We had to bury her of course. In a shoe box. In a "proper grave", the boys digging the hole. We held a little service around the graveside. I shed real tears, naturally—to think I was burying my little doll—and the others pretended to. Flowers were put on the grave, and then we did as the grown-ups did, walking slowly back, the men first, ladies following. As far as I know that doll is still there.

'A popular, if morbid, pastime was to visit households who had suffered a recent bereavement. There a group of us would gather at the door. At our knock, the door would be opened and we would gravely ask entry to view the body. We were welcomed inside and we would file silently upstairs to look at the corpse in its coffin. Then we would utter our thanks and file out again. But I still recall the shock I had when I saw the body of old Ann Jones with two pennies on top of her closed eyes. That scared me stiff and I never went corpse viewing again.

'At Easter, mother would boil a dozen or so eggs, dye them different colours and put names on them, for us and for our friends. We would distribute them proudly on Easter Monday morning, after which they were carefully carried to Pen Graig. There we would roll them down the grass slope, race after them and, after identifying our own, eat them in a great Easter feast.

'No-one in Harlech celebrated Guy Fawkes night. It was through an aunt in Liverpool that Harlech came to have its first firework display. She sent us a small box of fireworks a few days before the date, and on November 5th we all trooped to Pen Graig in great excitement. Perhaps there weren't many fireworks, two or three Catherine Wheels, a rocket or two, but to us, of course, it was a big event.

'As children we possessed one single golf club between us, a niblick. I had found it on the links at the Royal St. David's, and this was shared among a dozen of us. We'd all have a shot, always on the 15th green because it was largely hidden and no-one would see us. We would certainly have the luxury of more than one ball, however, for lost golf balls were plentiful. We'd perhaps go bathing first, then off we would all march—to the 15th green—with our one club. It is probably true to say that the many boys from Harlech who eventually became professional golfers in England, Canada and America learned their rough skills on the 15th green at the Royal St. David's, following this with caddying and then serving their time with the Harlech pro.'

The Circus came to town once a year. The children were always let off school and allowed to see the Grand Parade. They clapped as the elephants went by, and the clowns on stilts, and the beautifully plumed horses. 'That's about all we saw, however,' says Laura, 'for the threepence entrance fee was far beyond our means. This was just as true for our friends as it was for us, for Harlech wasn't a prosperous town. It was the English visitors who went to the circus, with their children and nannies.' 'We would watch them enviously as they went,' says Elsie. 'Afterwards we used to peep under the tent flap until the manager came with a stick and gave us a whack on the backside. That was part of the fun of course. Besides which it was worth it just to catch a glimpse of those lovely horses and to hear the shouting and the laughing at the clowns. Oh, we never missed the circus, even though we never saw more than a small part of it.'

The circus from Harlech Castle.

15

'*Calennig*' was a New Year custom. On New Year's Day children went to each house to wish the occupants a Happy New Year, and in return received nuts and fruits and miscellaneous oddments. 'We used to take a bag with us, hoping to fill it, but it never did seem to get full. Perhaps we ate all the gifts as we received them!' They would go the rounds in groups of three or four, often meeting other friends on the way, exchanging information and advice as to where to go. A big bonus would be if they received money. One house which was especially favoured was that of the castle caretaker, Richard Jones, who also ran a small business. All made a point of going there, for he always kept a pile of shining new pennies for New Year callers. 'I can see them now,' says Elsie, 'all along the hall shelf, gleaming and shining, one for each child that called. Of course there was always competition to get there early in case they'd all gone. But I don't believe anyone ever went without. Others, too, gave pennies, but Richard Jones's were special because they were so shiny and new. We never wanted to spend our precious coin because it looked so beautiful—but of course it didn't keep very long!'

As they received their little gifts they would chant:

C'lennig a ch'lennig, a Blwyddyn Newydd Dda,
Mr a Mrs, os gwelwch yn dda.

Roughly translated:

A New Year's gift if you please,
In return for our good wishes for a Happy New Year.

But if they didn't get anything they would chant:

C'lennig a ch'lennig, a Blwyddyn Newydd Ddrwg,
Gobeithio cewch lond tŷ o fwg.

We wish you a bad New Year,
And a house full of smoke.

But this was uttered well out of earshot!

A further treat lay in store on the first day back at school after the Christmas holidays. This was a visit from Mr. Ivor Jones, the headmaster's brother. He came on the first day, every year without fail, and they all looked forward to his visit because he brought with him two sacks, one filled with oranges and the other with apples. He would delve into these sacks and give each child an apple and an orange. 'We were thrilled to bits,' says Elsie. 'To us he was one of the finest of men and he certainly brought us joy on that special day. Perhaps children today would think nothing of it, but to us it was a highlight; oranges and apples were real luxuries in those days, for rarely did we have fruit in the house.'

'In the summer our cousins from Liverpool came to see us,' says Laura. 'They were a gay and lively lot and we used to look forward to their visits. In particular there would be great excitement in the household when our brother Jack and cousin Harold returned from sea. They always brought with them all the latest songs from America and they used to dance around the kitchen with mother.'

'Jack was very witty,' says Elsie. 'He came in one day after visiting a friend nearby, whose mother was preparing scones for tea and stirring the mixture in a bowl. Unfortunately there was a large dewdrop poised rather delicately on the end of her nose, just over the bowl. "Will you stay to tea, Jack?" she asked kindly. "Well," he replied, "it's according to how it drops." Fascinated, he watched while the dewdrop hung there for what seemed to be ages. "But, eventually it dropped right in," he said, "so I left."'

'Harold and he were both great practical jokers,' says Laura. 'On one visit home from sea Harold told mother that Jack had had a dreadful trip, facing mountainous seas and horrifying storms, and this had affected his mind, especially when money was mentioned. So he asked mother not to ask for her usual money until Jack was ready. Days and days passed, but Jack made no mention of it until mother began to get quite worried about finance. In the end she plucked up courage and began, "Jack dear, about the money . . ." But she got no further because he threw up his hands in the air and began to moan and shake. Thoroughly frightened, she shouted, "Oh, son! Oh, son! What have I done?" Then he and Harold began to laugh and, hugging her, said, "It's alright, it's alright, it's only a joke." At this Jack handed her his pay packet, which on this trip happened to be nearly double the usual amount. So all ended well.'

'Once, some years before this,' says Elsie, 'when Jack was quite young, our cousin Lily sent him up to the bedroom on the pretext of finding a book. As it was dark he began to look for a candle. "Oh, you don't want a candle," she said. "It's just by my bed." So up he went, but Lily had put a sweeping brush with a sheet over it against the door and as he opened it in the semi-darkness the brush fell on him and he screamed in fright. This time mother was cross, because it wasn't long after father's death and she thought it wrong of Lily to frighten a young boy in such a way.

'Next door to us was a tailor's shop, but we had the room directly above it, which was in fact Beattie's and my bedroom. From here we were able to peep down through cracks in the floorboards and watch Mr. Jones, the tailor, as we eavesdropped on his conversation with customers. This gave us a marvellous feeling of guilty excitement. One holiday Lily was staying with us. Always the possessor of an impish sense of humour, she suggested that we put pepper down through the floorboards. What a wonderful idea we thought, and so Beattie, Lily and I made our preparations. We waited for the shop to fill with customers and then we sprinkled over them what seemed to be huge quantities of pepper. Soon the whole shop was filled with the sound of great sneezing, luckily loud enough to cover our own convulsions of laughter! We were never found out!'

'One memorable summer,' says Laura, 'a friend of Harold's came from Liverpool to visit us for a week. He had the marvellous Lancashire name of Cobbledick, Dudley Cobbledick. He was no more than fifteen at the time, but his reputation for sheer mischief had preceeded him and wonderful stories about his escapades already enlivened our household. Apparently, on one occasion, after having his Saturday bath, he was leaning out of the bathroom window at his home in Liverpool, talking to friends. Dared by one to climb out and walk along the garden walls in the nude, he did so, prancing and balancing precariously to great shouts of encouragement and approval. When horrified neighbours knocked on Mrs. Cobbledick's door and told her that her son was parading around outside with nothing on, she at first didn't believe them, saying that Dudley was upstairs having his bath. However, once outside she saw her erring son and, amidst great hilarity and followed by a great crowd, young and old, she chased him up and down the street and, eventually, indoors!

18

'He was also the possessor of an accurate right arm. One day, his reputation now well established, he espied a particularly unfriendly neighbour, Mrs. Entwhistle, talking to the greengrocer, apparently complaining about him, for his name was mentioned more than once. Dudley stood at the door, watching. Mrs. Entwhistle suddenly turned, saw him and, mouth open, shouted, "There he is, the naughty . . ." but before she could finish, an egg, accurately aimed, hit her straight in the mouth. Almost in the same moment Dudley had turned and was off in a flash to escape the wrath of both Mrs. E. and the greengrocer for, after all, it *was* his egg!

'So, we awaited his visit, accompanied by his mother, with great anticipation. And he didn't disappoint. On the very first evening, while he and Jack were out playing in the street, Dudley kicked a ball straight through the open window of one of the cottages. Jack, on home territory, was more than a little embarrassed, but not Dudley. Bold as brass, he walked up to the front door and knocked. The lady came to the door.

"Please, missus, could I have me ball back?"

"Ball, ball, I haven't got your ball?"

"Yes you have," came the reply. "It's in your front parlour!"

'By the middle of the week he'd become friendly with a boy called Ieuan. Unfamiliar with Welsh names and being unable to wrap his tongue around this one he called at the house asking if "Thingee" could come out to play.

"Thingee," said his mother, "don't you dare call him Thingee. His name is Ieuan, and he's a very nice boy our Ieuan is."

"I haven't come here to ask about his character," said Dudley, "I just want to know if he can come out to play."

'On the final evening his mother sent him out for a pound of boiled ham for our supper. "But mind you get it without fat," she said. "You know I can't abide fat." I went with him to the shop but, with talking so much, he (and indeed I) forgot to ask for it without fat. Halfway home he suddenly remembered. He unwrapped it and found to his horror that it was extremely fatty. So, taking all the fat bits off he crammed a fistful into his mouth and re-wrapped the remainder. When he got home his mother soon saw that almost half had been devoured. Accusing him of being greedy and a thief to boot she

19

packed him off to bed without his supper. However, after I told her what had happened and we'd all had a good laugh she relented and decided to give him some sandwiches (the offending ham) and milk. But, not wanting to lose face, she asked me to take them upstairs and not to let him know that she was responsible. So, I quietly crept upstairs and knocked on the bedroom door.

"Yes?"

"It's me, Laura. I've brought some ham sandwiches for you."

"Does mother know?"

"No, I got them off the kitchen table."

"Then you can take them straight down again. No more stolen goods for me."

Dudley Cobbledick. What a character! We did miss him when he went back to Liverpool.'

Elsie now takes up the story: 'One of our most pleasant jaunts was to go to concerts. There would invariably be a singer and a pianist. Of course we used to love to ape their mannerisms and try to imitate them when we got home.

'We didn't possess such a thing as a piano—indeed there were only about four households in the whole of Harlech with a piano at that time. But what we did have was a treadle sewing machine. There was a box top and the side came out, and that to us was the "piano". Beattie would draw up a chair, prop mother's song book in front of her and "play" with many flourishes and great panache. I would sing, standing on a little stool still dressed in my concert-going clothes. Whoever we had seen in that evening's concert I would imitate, male or female, with Beattie accompanying me with all the little twiddly bits. Mother would be sitting there with a book in her lap, occasionally giving a little laugh. At such moments we would turn around. "What are you laughing at, mother?" "Oh, something funny in the book I'm reading," she would reply, but I know now that it wasn't. Back we would go to our performance, my sister turning the leaves with deft fingers while I sang with my book stretched out in front. In those days all singers had a book, whether they looked at it or not. It was just something they held.

'I sang lustily, with all the right grimaces. I suppose mother would go upstairs to bed with sides sore with suppressed laughter. It was

20

always my task to sing, Beattie's to play the piano, and I must say she seemed to play well although all you heard, of course, was the tap of fingertips on wood! It was all great fun. It was no sewing machine to us. It was a piano, my footstool was the stage and I sang my heart out.

'I used to visit a house which had a real piano,' continues Elsie, 'and that was the house of Police Sergeant Davies in Top Dre (literally, 'top of the town'). A widower for many years, he brought his spinster sister to live there to look after his only child, Ella. Ella's nickname was 'Ella Spots', not because she had pimples but because, dressed always in pretty frocks, she worried dreadfully if she sustained the merest spot or mark on them. "Oh dear," she'd say, "that dirty spot will make Auntie cross with me."

'She was a charming little pianist and, after we'd had our tea, always a nice tea on a table laid with a dainty lace cloth, her doting father would say, "Ella, dear, now play the piano and Elsie will sing." She would always play the same little tune, "Won't you buy my pretty flowers?" often the first piano piece that children learned in those days, while I would sing:

> Underneath the gaslight's glitter
> Stands a little fragile girl
> Heedless of the night winds bitter
> As they round about her whirl.
>
> There are many sad and weary
> In this pleasant world of ours
> Crying out in tearful pleading
> Won't you buy my pretty flowers?

Sergeant Davies and his sister would clap us both as we blushingly sat down, the evening then ending pleasantly with the four of us playing "Ludo".'

Indoor activities such as these tended to be winter ones, of course, for outdoor games were restricted during the dark evenings. If they *were* out on such nights the children would gather under the street lamps' comforting glow to play hop-scotch or hide-and-seek, made more exciting by the darkness that lay beyond those pools of delight, until, one by one, they would be called home.

21

CHAPTER 3

Schooldays

'At school I sat next to John Edmund Evans,' says Elsie. 'For years I thought I'd marry him because he was good to me, for he used to let me copy his answers.' She pauses. 'My goodness, that was over eighty years ago . . .'

In those days children left school at fourteen, sometimes before then if parents needed their help at home. Educational provision was lamentably low. Poor educational standards and illiteracy were prevalent throughout Wales. In 1914 there were only forty-one Welsh Grammar School pupils for every 1,000 in Elementary Schools, a far lower figure than in either England or Scotland. For the vast majority of Welsh children education was limited and was poorly provided for at elementary, secondary and higher levels. Harlech School was no different. It was built as a Board School in 1874, largely due to the influence and backing of the philanthropist Samuel Holland. For sixteen years Liberal MP for Merioneth, having made his money in the Blaenau Ffestiniog slate industry, he was closely involved in many good works in Harlech and elsewhere in the county.

Harlech schoolchildren at the beginning of the century.

Dudley Maidment collection

'Despite his efforts, however, Harlech School wasn't a good school,' says Elsie. 'Certainly in the years before the First World War there seemed no real attempt to teach and little interest was shown by the staff. There was quite often blatant neglect and clever children who were handicapped by being poor never got a chance. There were seven classes in all, an Infants' class and Forms One to Six. Classes were overcrowded because families in Harlech were large, and some had as many as six or seven children. Two families in a village some five miles away had twenty-six children between them and all of them came to school. Most children walked a long way, many from the upland farms high on the hills. They trudged to school in all sorts of weather, bringing their lunches with them, often a primitive meal of bread and dripping and a bottle of cold tea. This would have to sustain them until they got home in the evening.'

There was little Welsh taught—perhaps a little translation occasionally. Educational Commissioners and Schools' Inspectors attacked the Welsh language as an obstacle to culture and enlightenment. Although Welsh was spoken as the first language in homes and in the playground few were able to read it or write it because the teaching medium was English. They were taught in English, from English books. In certain parts of Wales, until late in the nineteenth century, the 'Welsh Not' was officially used to discourage pupils from speaking Welsh. This device was a piece of wood with a loop of string hung around the neck and a pupil could only get rid of it by passing it to another caught speaking Welsh. At the end of the week the unfortunate pupil with it last around his neck would be beaten.

Regular attendance at school was looked upon as being of the utmost importance. The School Attendance Officer (or 'children's policeman' as he was commonly called in Harlech—'plismon plant' in some sort of half-Welsh) was a regular visitor to school and home to check on truancy. 'My own attendance, however,' says Elsie, 'was always good and I still possess a prize book given to me for consistency in this respect.' There was, nevertheless, still some flexibility allowed in attendance. Children were given a day off for Harvest Thanksgiving, a half day for Harlech Fair Day and for the visit of the circus, although, surprisingly, there was no allowance for St. David's Day. Farmers' children got time off at haytime and children who had suffered family bereavement often stayed home until after the funeral with the Headmaster himself usually attending.

Another regular visitor was the 'nit nurse' who would carefully inspect the children's hair. 'While she found some in a poor and dirty condition,' says Elsie, 'I received compliments for the cleanliness of my own. Every night mother would comb it and brush it, and Beattie's too, until both heads would shine. Once, however, she did find nits in my hair and, horrified, she crushed moth balls into fine powder and rubbed it in. The napthalene seemed to cure the condition though I went to bed smelling to high heaven!

'The state of general health as I recall was reasonably good. School was only ever fully closed twice in my time there, once for a week for an outbreak of scarlet fever (*y clefyd coch*) and once for a similar period for diphtheria.'

As much importance was attached to promptness of arrival as to attendance and both girls and boys were caned for lateness. There were always two bells, the first rung as a five-minute warning, the second causing the school gates to be soundly shut.

Lessons were strictly formalised. There was never any physical training, no games, not even exercise periods. English was divided into Composition, Spelling and Dictation; Geography was a listing of cities, countries, mountains, rivers and lakes; History generally a repetition of dates and studies of Kings and Queens. Calligraphy was thought important and involved the careful copying, in copper-plate handwriting, of words and sentences from the blackboard.

'The only class in which we ever really learned anything at all,' says Elsie, 'was the Headmaster's class, for Daniel Jones, solely amongst his staff, took a real interest in his pupils, although Miss Ellis, of the infants, was much liked.'

Laura agrees. 'Daniel Jones was always fair and understanding. He was a wonderful teacher of history and he brought it to life. I remember one day in particular when he called me out in front of the class to show that Saxon hair was very much like my own—long and golden. He had us perform little scenes, unusual in those days—a Roman encampment, Saxon villagers building wattle and daub houses, or a Tudor household preparing to meet the King on a hunting visit.

'He used to take us also to the famous and mysterious pre-Celtic hut

24

circles in the uplands above Harlech which to this day we call *Cytiau Gwyddelod*, or Irish huts. Higher still we climbed the "Roman Steps", a stairway of several hundred stones, half a mile long. Although there are many Roman remains in this part of Wales he told us that these steps were medieval in origin, not Roman, and were possibly laid to make the crossing easier for Welsh cattle drovers on their long journey across the mountains and on to English market towns.'

'Mr. Jones started our interest in birds,' says Elsie, 'and he warned of severe punishment being given to those who went bird-nesting. His classroom was a joy to walk into because the walls were lined with pictures of birds, flowers and trees. Another of the pleasant things about the Headmaster's class was that we used the famous "copy books" and had pen and ink, paper and "real" pencils, unlike the other classes where we used only slates and slate pencils.

The 'Roman Steps'.

Dudley Maidment collection

25

'He was a noted botanist, nationally known as an authority on mosses. I think we realised this even then. It always caused a stir of excitement and pleasure in the class when he said, "Now, boys and girls, put away your books and let us go and find out for ourselves." I still retain my love of nature from these visits,' she continues. 'We were scattered on the hill-side to gather specimens of flowers and mosses to take back to school to copy. It was in this way that I learned to recognize red and white campion, ragged robin, stitchwort and the now rarely-to-be-seen birds' foot trefoil—so delicate and beautiful.

'Perhaps in class he wasn't really strict enough. On many afternoons in winter he would have a nap in front of the fire, his last words before going to sleep being, "Now, all read your books and settle down there." We knew that those words were the prelude to his soon being asleep in front of the fire, feet on the fire-guard and with his stick on the desk as a somewhat ineffective warning. Soon there would be a rumpus. The boys would be fighting, the girls would have their hair stuffed in inkwells and our crisp white pinafores would be covered in blue-black stains.

'One day Will Thomas brought a mouse to school. Now Will was a bit of a bully and we were all frightened of him. During the afternoon nap he turned the mouse loose, amidst laughter from the boys and screams from the girls, enough on this occasion to wake up old DJ. He got his stick and walloped the desk, obtaining immediate silence. He asked what all the din was about. We told him, and the boys were sent to find the mouse while the girls were asked who had been responsible. Will Thomas warned us not to tell, but I did tell, because for once I was more frightened of Daniel Jones than of Will as old DJ walloped the desk yet again. "It was Will Thomas, sir," I piped. Poor Will had two strokes of the cane on each hand. After leaving school that afternoon I ran miles the other way to avoid him and the inevitable retribution, but in doing so it made me late for tea and I got a walloping in turn!

'One day in late spring Will came to us as we were playing on the rocks. He'd found a bird's nest with five chicks in it. He had these chicks in his pocket, and in front of our horrified eyes he took them out and cut off their heads with a penknife. Someone told DJ the following day—not yours truly this time—and immediately, mindful

26

of his dire warnings about bird protection, he took Will into the playground, told him to take down his trousers and thrashed him hard across his bare buttocks. Will, however, was a strong lad, and brave, and he didn't let out a single whimper. But he didn't go near a bird's nest after that, and the bullying stopped also. He and I met many years later and we talked over our schooldays. He remembered the caning and we laughed over it. He had developed into a fine person, and did much good work in town and chapel. He was well-liked and respected. School had done him no harm, at least.'

Elsie continues, 'The teacher for Form Four was Mrs. Bevers. She was a very strict disciplinarian. She ground your head with her knuckles when you made a mistake. "You booby," she'd say, or "You idiot." She ran the sewing class on Friday afternoons, for which we had to take our own materials. I always took a pillowslip. My stitching was so poor that mother used to ask me if I used a poker! Once we were asked to take material to school to make a pinafore, but mother couldn't afford any, nor could Mrs. Owen find any for my friend Maria. So Mrs. Bevers made us both stand in the corner where we had to mend chemises.

'While she was out, Maria and I put them on and went on our knees to imitate the vicar at prayer, much to the amusement of all! But she came back and caught us, threatening to put us in front of the boys' drawing class next door. That would have been the biggest humiliation, but we were put back in the corner instead and made to wear those chemises for the rest of the lesson!

'She once caught me playing "tick" in the cloakroom after school. I bumped straight into her and she held me firmly in an iron grip while my friends took their chance to make their escape. When I wouldn't give her their names, saying rather lamely that I didn't know who they were, she kept me behind to write 100 times, "My name is Elsie Williams and I told a lie."

'Mrs. Bevers just didn't seem to bother with pupils whom she knew wouldn't be able to afford to go to the County School at Barmouth. Many pupils did like her and respect her, but I didn't. She had no patience with me and I had no love for her.

'However, some time after I left school and shortly after the sad news came through that her only son, Gwilym, a Lieutenant in the

Royal Welch Fusiliers, had been killed in France, I was walking at dusk a little outside the town when I saw a figure lying at the side of the road. I went over and, to my surprise, found that it was Mrs. Bevers. She was moaning and obviously in great distress and I ran to the doctor's house nearby for help. She was taken home and though at first very ill she recovered well. Later I called to see her and she held my hand and whispered, *"Diolch yn fawr, Elsie"* (Thank you very much, Elsie). We had a long chat and got closer to each other than we ever had at school.'

CHAPTER 4

The Shops

The main ladies' shop in Harlech belonged to Johnny Morris. 'Siop Johnny Morris' was well-known throughout the town. 'It was rarely, however, that our family bought anything there,' says Laura, 'because mother made all our clothes. She was a clever needlewoman and she made some quite beautiful things.'

'Yes,' agrees Elsie. 'I remember particularly a wonderful *crepe-de-chine*, long-waisted frock she made for me. I can vividly recall the prim and proud feeling I had when I wore it to church for the first time. In fact, it was made out of a nightdress that Lady Gladys Winchilsea had given to mother. I was the envy of the other girls because it had belonged to Lady Gladys, though I doubt if I ever said it had been a nightdress!'

At Christmas time the local children used to gaze in awe at the brightly-lit shops with their decorations, although perhaps by today's standards they would be poor indeed. But for them it was marvellous to see handkerchiefs with 'Merry Christmas' embroidered on them, or a lighted candle surrounded by holly, or a pig's head in the butcher's window, with an orange in its mouth.

'There was one toy shop,' says Elsie, 'owned by Margiad Williams and it was full of beautiful dolls at Christmas, large and small. We used to press our faces against the window to take in as much as we could in one enraptured gaze. The windows were usually lit by paraffin lamps, and there was a sort of magic about such light that is hard to imagine today. We knew we would never get dolls such as they displayed in that window. They were for children from wealthier families, but it was still lovely to see them. By the time Christmas came we had given them all different names—the names that we would call them had they been ours. We would call out, "She's mine," or "I pick that one," and then there would be a quarrel as to who was first. Nevertheless, it is a remembered joy. In some garbled half-English, half-Welsh the magic phrase was "*Fost i fi*"—meaningless really, but we assumed to be "First (choice) for me".

'I remember one Christmas in particular. It was because, for once, I *had* been given a beautiful doll and cradle, and Beattie received a doll and bath, gifts from Lady Winchilsea's personal maid, Mrs. West. Both dolls were made of wax. I adored this doll and used to take her to bed with me, but one night a most awful thing happened. I must have slept on her, for in the morning she had no face—it was just a flat, squashed mess. I broke my heart.

'In the window of Griffith Jones Williams' shoe shop was a wax woman feathering a goose, though quite what she was doing in a shoe shop we didn't know. She had a bonnet tied around her chin and the goose hung down from her knees. Every Christmas she would sit there, plucking this goose. Flying from her quick fingers, the feathers would disappear and then appear again by some magic powers beyond our ken. We used to watch this for what seemed to be hours on end, wondering where the feathers went. Every so often the shopkeeper would wind her up, and on went the magical performance. It was the placing of the goose woman in the shoe shop window, above all else, which persuaded us that Christmas was once again drawing near. I believe that this little figure, still working her fingers away, lasted right up to the years after the Second World War.'

Sam and Jane Williams kept an ironmongery shop, 'Gwalia Stores', although Sam himself was also head postman at the Post Office. A strong socialist at a time when most of the town was staunchly Liberal, he was also anti-monarchist and an objector to English upper class visitors. Each autumn these visitors used to leave behind clothing and other items for a jumble sale, the proceeds from which went to church funds. 'At times most of Harlech seemed to be at these jumble sales,' says Elsie. 'One day Sam's younger daughter and my close friend Ann ("Ann Jane Sam" as she was often called to different-iate her from numerous other "Ann Janes") bought a shawl at one of these sales. When she brought it home her father became very cross. He didn't want any of his children wearing "aristocratic cast-offs" and he told her to take it back. Ann, who could have been no more than twelve at the time, flared at her father and said, "You won't allow me to wear their clothes, yet you don't refuse their custom in

High Street, Harlech.

your shop and make me carry *your* goods to *their* houses!'' She floun-ced out, leaving him with mouth wide open!

'On one occasion,' continues Elsie, 'during the Investiture of the Prince of Wales in 1911, photographs of the Prince were displayed in many Harlech shop windows. Ann fell in love with one such photo-graph, beautifully framed, in Margiad Williams' toy shop, costing 2/6d, a large sum in those days. She went home and found that she had just enough cash in her money box, so back she went to the shop to buy it. Again her father objected and he forbade her to have the photograph in his sight. So Ann took Edward upstairs to her bed-room, kissing him fondly before she went to sleep each night, but taking care to hide him safely in a drawer before she went to school each day!'

Lewis Foster Edwards—FE—was a kindly red-faced man who, with his wife, ran 'Cambrian House' in the Castle Square, rented from Lord Winchilsea at a cost of about £17 a year. It was a shop that sold everything from bread to marbles. 'Siop Foster' was popular

31

because he was such a pleasant man, always good humoured and with a kind word for everyone. He was a familiar and popular sight on the streets in his black apron with a basket over his arm carrying goods to various houses. FE also had a little sea cabin by the golf course which sold golfballs and clubs.

John Ivor Jones kept a grocery shop, 'Gwyndy Stores' (White House Stores). It was without doubt a superior establishment, and it catered for the numerous English visitors who came each summer.

'Mother was very fond of Cleeves butter,' says Elsie, 'the best kind of English creamery butter. One day she sent me to fetch some; she would have no other and we wouldn't dare accept any substitute. Except on this day, when the assistant told me there wasn't any Cleeves butter in stock . . . I did. "How many times must I tell you," said mother when I got back, "that no other butter will do. Take it back, please."

'Despite my protestations that I would be late for school back I had to go, my mother pointing out with some logic that the more I argued the later I would be. So back I ran with this alternative but unacceptable butter. The assistant who had served me had a somewhat sour disposition and, I suspect, wondered by what right mother wanted Cleeves butter, for she was one of the poorer members of the community and Cleeves butter was usually requested only by English visitors. Certainly it *was* expensive, but Cleeves butter, like heat and light, was one of life's little luxuries that mother allowed herself. I stood outside the window for quite some time, nervous of entering. Eventually Mr. Jones himself came from the back of the shop and I darted in to explain that mother wanted Cleeves butter and that she'd rather wait until it came in. "But we have some," he said. I explained that his assistant had said there was none in stock. "Nonsense," he replied. "There's plenty." He went up to the assistant and I think told her off. She gave me the butter in a huff but, too much in a hurry to be pleased, I ran all the way home with that half pound of precious butter. I remember that mother was cross about the affair because she felt slighted.

'A smaller grocer's shop was kept by mother's greatest friend in Harlech, Elin Owen. She was a great wit and always full of fun. When Maria, her daughter and my best friend, used to ask for a ha'penny, she would answer, *"Cei, os caf i un ar lawr a neb wedi ei cholli."* (Yes, if I find one on the floor and no-one has lost it). The plaintive reply would always come, "O, Mam."

'I used to love bread and treacle. We never had treacle at home, only syrup, because mother as a child had been given treacle for medicine, laced with brimstone. But to us it was a treat when we had it at Mrs. Owen's. She would ask us what shape we wanted her to make with the treacle—*"Llun mwnci neu dy enw?"* (A picture of a monkey or your name?). Mrs. Owen had poor schooling and couldn't really write, but she would dribble something on the bread and clap the other piece on top so quickly that I never knew whether it was my name or a picture of a monkey! Though I always wanted my name. Then she would dismiss us with *"Dos i Patagonia"* (Go to Patagonia) or "Nova Scotia" or "Hong Kong". We wondered where these places were, and often thought she was making them up. But, of course, they came from sailor folk, for three of her brothers were seafarers.

'For all her lack of education and wayward ability at English, she was a warm and jolly woman. Once, seeing Beattie with a dollop of cream on her face, she asked of mother in a phrase I never forgot, "What she try to do, Mrs. Williams, is she try to shav?" We loved to go there, always.'

Every Tuesday and Friday Elsie and Beattie, along with other Harlech children, took home-prepared dough to Mr. Hughes' bakery in Grogan Terrace for baking. 'His cleanliness left a lot to be desired, a fact which didn't entirely please mother,' says Beattie. 'But there was no alternative. However, the bread was beautifully baked (it cost 1½d a time) and the overhanging crust which we called, for no apparent reason, *"llo bach"* (little calf) would often be broken off and eaten before we got home.'

'He used to put a "tally" on the dough to mark and identify it,' says Elsie. 'But we were warned by mother that Mr. Hughes was not to put a tally on our dough because of his lack of hygiene. She herself would put "AW" (Amelia Williams) on it as her own identifying mark. But he would still insist on putting his own tally on, and we were too frightened to argue too much with him. Through a cleft palate he would answer our meagre protestations:

33

"Dwed wrth dy fam bod yn rhaid i mi roi tali arno" (Tell your mother I have to put a tally on).
"Mae'n henw ni ar top, Mr. Hughes" (Our name is on the top, Mr. Hughes).
"'Sdim ots, mae'n rhaid i mi" (It doesn't matter. I have to). We used to try our best to scrape the tally mark off. But if we did mother would want to know if we'd washed our hands. She had a special muslin cloth in which we took the dough and fetched the bread. No-one else did this and we were terribly embarrassed about it. And then the loaf would still be thoroughly scraped with the bread knife as soon as we got in.'

Apart from selling bread Mr. and Mrs. Hughes also sold confectionery. There were numerous bottles of different sizes, filled with sweets of all kinds. Mrs. Hughes, who looked after the shop, was easily confused and the children would love to add to her confusion by changing their minds again and again over choosing their sweets—liquorice, cocoa chips, sherbert or lucky dip. On Saturday mornings there would be 'mixed sweets', the remnants from each bottle. They came cheaper and were therefore greatly popular.

'Siop Mari Thomas' was another sweet shop. Mari kept the shop open in the evenings so that the farm boys would have somewhere to go after their day's work, to drink ginger-beer and gossip. A lovely old lady, she brought up from childhood her elder daughter's slighly simple illegitimate son. Morris was constantly teased at school that Mari was his grandmother, not his mother, until one day he came rushing into the house in sheer exasperation and said, *"Mam i mi wyt ti, 'te, Nain?"* (You're my mother, aren't you, Gran?).

'A hut in the grounds of Bron-y-Graig was rented from the Earl of Winchilsea by a certain Mr. Davies,' says Elsie. 'In this hut he made excellent ginger-beer in bottles with glass stoppers. "Mr. Davies ginger-beer", as he was called, was not a native of Harlech and he was a rather reserved, lonely man. Nevertheless, we got to know him quite well, for he lodged with our aunt in her house in the town, Clogwyn Villa, and we found him to be a gentle, kindly person. The boys of the town bought ginger-beer from him at a shilling a box, re-sold at a good profit in the castle grounds to summer visitors!

'The paint and wallpaper shop was kept by Bob Parry. A jolly man

34

of whom mother was very fond, he suffered a chronic skin complaint, possibly from the amount of lead in the paint in those days, and which seemed to resist all normal medicines. Mother gave him a pot of her ointment to try and, after two or three applications it seemed to do the trick, for the blemishes disappeared completely. In his appreciation he papered our kitchen walls!'

The main tailor's shop, gentlemen's and ladies', belonged to Huw Jones of Porkington Terrace. A life-long bachelor, he was small, delicate in his movements and lame, although he danced well and indeed for many years taught ballroom dancing in the town. A superb craftsman, he returned to Harlech after some years in Savile Row in order to open his own shop, where, in due course, many of Harlech's wealthier families became regular customers. 'After going into service,' says Laura, 'for the first time in my life I was able to afford good clothes and my very first suit was made by Huw Jones. In pale grey with dark grey piping, a cut-away jacket and hobble skirt with black buttons off-centre, it cost less than £3. It was a lovely suit but what made it more special was the pleasure I had in going there, because his unfailing courtesy and charming behaviour, always addressing me politely as "Miss Williams", gave me, and I am sure all his customers, a warm and welcoming feeling.'

Hats were made by two local milliners, one of whom worked with Johnny Morris the draper and the other with Mr. Griffiths at the Post Office. They were kept constantly busy, for no lady went hatless in those days. A Miss Arthur had a workshop at the rear of Johnny Morris's shop and took under her wing a number of young girls as apprentice milliners. 'I worked with Miss Arthur for a year,' says Beattie, 'learning the art of elegant design under her expert tuition, before I went to London at the age of sixteen to become a milliner myself.'

'Miss Arthur was friendly with mother,' says Elsie, 'and I remember one particular hat that she made for her, a large swathed toque in dove grey satin, with a black ostrich feather that Jack had brought home from one of his overseas voyages. A most beautiful hat, it sat on a stand in the shop window for some days before mother collected it. Mrs. Jones, the doctor's wife, fell in love with it and asked Miss Arthur to sell it to her. When Miss Arthur said that it had been

35

made for Mrs. Amelia Williams Mrs. Jones rather presumptiously said that Mrs. Williams wouldn't mind if she, Mrs. Jones, bought it instead. Miss Arthur, offended for her own sake as well as mother's, replied haughtily that it was "reserved". Mother wore that hat with a natural elegance that few, for all their money, would have been able to match.

'The little road where we lived was called Pentre'r Efail (Smithy's Village),' continues Elsie, 'and No. 3 across the road from where we lived was the actual smithy, selling ornamental ironwork, gates and so on. Mr. Morris, the smith, also made hoops and gave them away free for the boys to play with. Horses were shod daily and the constant burning left a nasty odour hanging in the air. We loathed it, but I was very friendly with the Morris family. They were better off than we were, with better food—and a piano! We used to sit outside, sometimes on the window-sill, while their eldest daughter Maggie had lessons from the vicar's sister who taught organ and piano. Maggie used to thump away, and how we envied her. We thought she was a great pianist, although later on we found out that she was pretty hopeless. When I think of it now I realise that she could hardly play a hymn through!

'The Morris family always kept two pigs, one for Christmas and one for the first autumn month with an "R" in it. School wasn't very far away, just up the hill and, twice in the autumn term—once in September and once in December—while we were doing our school work we used to hear high-pitched screams as the pigs were being slaughtered, a terrible and frightening noise.

'Mrs. Morris was an awful tease.' One day when I returned home from school she asked me and her youngest daughter Annie to come down to the pantry. I wasn't keen, but I wasn't brave enough to decline and when we got there we found a dead pig hanging up with a bonnet on its head! I screamed and ran straight upstairs and across the street, home. Mother was cross with Mrs. Morris for playing such a trick, but she was always full of fun, and kind and generous with it. Her kindness to mother was shown by her being one of the first to be given a piece of pork whenever they killed a pig.

'Every Sunday Mrs. Morris would bake a large cake. We called it *"cacen wy"* (egg cake) because it was always made with six or more eggs. Each Sunday Annie and I would cut ourselves two enormous pieces to take outside to eat, but never once did her mother tell us off or indicate that she knew. It tasted like heaven.

'Mr. Morris was just as much a tease as his wife. He was a large man and he frightened the wits out of me by his very presence. I used to look in at the window before calling for Annie, and if Mr. Morris was there I would creep quietly away. He seemed to know that I was in awe of him. More than once he said he would like to marry my mother, and the very thought terrified me. "When Mrs. Morris dies," he used to say, "I'm going to marry your mother." This awful possibility would appear likely when, during winter evenings at home and we were playing quietly, mother would sigh as she went through our clothes, stitching and sewing, and she would murmur that really she would have to find a new husband to support us all. This terrified me even further, and I used to go down on my knees and beg her not to marry James Morris!'

CHAPTER 5

The Beach

The Harlech beach is one of the loveliest in all Britain, five or six miles of firm, golden sand, safe bathing, with long rolling breakers. Behind are sand dunes forty to fifty feet high, vast areas of play for tick and hide-and-seek, with hiding places that could hardly be bettered anywhere.

On Saturdays and holidays in high summer the children of Harlech virtually lived on the beach. On bright sunny mornings they would march down, armed with drinks in bottles, sometimes only water, occasionally cold tea. Those that wanted to show off took 'lemon cali', crystals which when mixed with water gave a somewhat nauseous yellow liquid. For food there would be jam sandwiches, perhaps a bun or scone from the bakery, 'Although in excitement and hunger we'd usually scoffed the lot before we got halfway!' says Elsie. 'About a dozen boys and girls used to go—the "Pentre'r Efail lot" as we were called, to distinguish us from the "Gorffwysfa types" from the other end of town, with whom, like youngsters the world over, we never mixed.'

Harlech Beach.

Author's collection

Enjoying a paddle!

Dudley Maidment collection

When they were in the water the sexes generally separated, for the girls bathed in their knickers and the boys either in pants or in the nude, because no-one possessed such a luxury as a bathing costume. 'One day, however,' says Elsie, 'I did find a costume which we assumed had belonged to a visitor. It was dark blue, with a tied neck, half-sleeved. It was much too big for me, of course, but I thought I looked the "Belle of the Beach" in it. In fact, I must have looked a real "cut", especially with a cap on my head to save getting my hair wet. The cap was rubber, bought cheaply at "Siop Johnny Morris", with a frill all around. The girls were jealous of the costume, but I used to let them borrow it in turns, and they all wore it with equal pride. I'm sure we amused many visitors as we paraded around. I'm sure, too, we must still be on many a photograph somewhere.'

In and out of the sea they would go, all day long, then they would walk the length of the beach to reach the so-called 'Zig-Zag', a winding cliff path. Here at the foot of the cliff were clusters of rocks and numerous small pools, filled partly by sea water but also fed by fresh water streams that flowed from the hills behind the town. Amongst the rocks were colonies of limpets and periwinkles. It was the boys' task to prise these away, while the girls collected fresh water in an old tin bucket made by Mr. Morris the smith and brought by his daughter Annie. Four big stones were collected to make a grate, together with rushes for a fire. Limpets and periwinkles would be washed and then put into the bucket to be boiled. Afterwards, in the twilight, they would gather around, armed with pins, to eat freshly cooked seafood before, finally, at the end of the long day, walking slowly up the 'Zig-Zag' and making their way home.

During the summer months numerous tents dotted Harlech beach and its sandhills. Many of them had a gay appearance with colourful stripes in reds or greens or yellows. In the evenings, after the visitors had gone, the children would untie the flaps and go inside to dry themselves and get dressed.

There were a number of beach huts, too, most of which would be locked up in the evenings. 'Rarely could entry be forced here,' says Beattie, 'but at least they gave us shelter from the wind when we stood behind them to change. However, one particular morning four of us were delighted to find that one, belonging to the Mores of Crown Lodge, had been left unlocked. With no sign of the Mores around we all trooped inside to undress, putting our clothes neatly in the corner, and off we ran to the sea. When we returned we were shocked to find all our clothes scattered outside on the sand. Thinking the Mores had arrived we guiltily picked everything up but while we were doing so the door of the hut burst open and there stood a man, absolutely naked. Transfixed only for a moment by horror, quick as lightning we shot off into the dunes to hide and sort ourselves out. While nervously chatting and dressing we saw Police Sergeant Davies riding his bicycle down the narrow path leading to the shore. It was most unusual to see him down there, and we debated whether or not to tell him about the incident. It was decided that I, being the cheeky one, should do so. To my astonishment he thanked me for telling him. He told us that he was on his way to look for this man as others had complained about his behaviour on the beach, and that we had helped him considerably by giving his exact location. Nevertheless he still turned and came back to give us a little lecture not to use other people's property without consent! Later on, a rumour went around that the man was a German aristocrat and a guest in one of the big houses. He looked German we thought, but a looney one!'

'Something else regularly "borrowed",' says Elsie, 'was the Graves' family raft, but I remember the very last time I did that. We were sitting there chatting, boys and girls together on this occasion, our legs dangling in the water, when someone shouted that it had come off its anchor and was drifting out to sea. In my panic I jumped into the water and immediately went under. The minister's son, John Prosser Davies, realised my terror as I sank and struggled and he literally dragged me up by the hair. Luckily I wasn't wearing my famous cap that day, but it made me frightened of the sea from that day on.'

'One winter afternoon during the Great War,' says Beattie, 'a group of us were walking along the beach. There had been a terrible storm the previous night and there was a lot of debris washed ashore, obviously from a shipwreck. We were amazed to find rotten oranges and apples all over the place alongside barrels, drums full of oil and bits of furniture. We were told by Sergeant Davies to leave the oil drums alone, as they were Government property. As if we would have been able to move them! A little further along we found what we thought was a dead whale but we were told afterwards that it was a dolphin. To us it looked huge, certainly big enough to be a whale. When we returned a short while later we found many local farmers cutting it up and putting great pieces of its flesh on wheelbarrows. We were horrified and saddened. It seemed such an undignified end to such a massive, yet pathetic creature.'

41

'We played a lot in the warm water pools left by the outgoing tide,' says Elsie. 'Religion played its part in our beach games, too, for in these pools we would play "Baptisms". Once I played the "Minister" and in "baptising" one rather big girl *("Yn enw'r Tad, y Mab a'r Ysbryd Glân"*—In the name of the Father, Son and Holy Ghost) she pulled me over so hard that we both went head over heels, much to the amusement of all! It wasn't always religion though. Once, when someone asked the cause of some obnoxious smell (it was probably seaweed), I said, *"Cranc wedi taro rhech"* (A crab that's farted). It brought the house down!

'It was such great fun. The boys would hide our clothes and we would have to go chasing them for miles to get them back. But it was all very innocent. There was never a suggestion of anything improper—probably because we knew them so well, sitting next to them in school as we did. They were lovely boys, and they were lovely golden days.'

CHAPTER 6

Golf

The Royal St. David's Golf Club is set in some of the most beautiful scenery in the British Isles. It has been 'Royal' since the time of Edward VII (since 1908), although he was Patron as far back as 1896. King George V became Patron in 1910 and Edward VIII played there when he was Prince of Wales, becoming Club Captain in 1934.

Mr. W. H. More.

The Club was formed in 1894 and began in a strange way. A comparative newcomer to Harlech in those days was Mr. W. H. More, Crown Agent for Wales and Monmouth, and one day he saw from the window of his house overlooking the Morfa a man hurling some sort of missile, retrieving it, then doing it all over again. Curiosity prompted him to go down to look more closely and soon he became engaged in conversation with the stranger. The visitor told him that he was Harold Finch-Hatton, younger brother of the Earl of Winchilsea, that he had spent some years in Australia, sheep farming, where he had learnt the art of boomerang throwing which he was now practising. Later Finch-Hatton remarked that the turf on which they stood would be ideal for golf. Finch-Hatton then returned to London.

Some time later another visitor, a fashionable West End doctor, told More that the Morfa would make fine links and that golf would be a great attraction in an otherwise dull place like Harlech. More then wrote to Finch-Hatton telling him of that conversation and, to his astonishment, he received a telegram the next day saying, 'Do not stir a sod. Have made a plan of the links. Coming tomorrow.' On his arrival he and More marched around, armed with stakes, with Finch-Hatton jabbing one after another into the ground, saying 'First tee here', or 'Good place for first green', to the complete bewilderment of More who hadn't the first concept of what the game of golf was all about.

Finch-Hatton went away the next day, leaving the plan, saying, 'Now you can get going. Let me know when you start work and I'll come down again. Put me down for a tenner.' One can imagine More's dismay. Here he was, a newcomer to the area, knowing nothing about the game and being told virtually to start a golf club from scratch. He must have virtually shrugged his shoulders and said to himself, 'Well, let's begin.'

The first moves were to meet the local tenants and to bargain for the land in a mixture of Welsh and English. He explained that the game was played with a stick and ball and that no harm would be done to the grazing land (such things as bunkers being foreign territory to him). One of the tenants puzzled More by asking about 'the ponies', but it turned out that he thought they were talking about polo! With some

44

rough and tough bargaining More settled the lot for £27 per annum and a celebratory meal at a local inn.

The next items on More's list were the obtaining of funds, finding members and acquiring some knowledge of the game, all of which he was able to obtain from a small club at neighbouring Barmouth. There was a nine-hole course there, where somewhat casual golf was played by local county gentlemen who spent most of their time eating and drinking. There was a quite fierce Hon. Sec., Thomas Best, then Chief Constable of the County, who usually disqualified from membership those he didn't like. By frequent visits to this interesting club More was able to acquire some knowledge of the game, though it was no doubt somewhat slanted. Furthermore, despite the ire of Thomas Best, he was able to seduce some of the members to join the new club and at the same time hand over a guinea in subscription fees. The Barmouth club was soon to collapse in debt but its cheerful ex-members agreed that their Gold Cup should be transferred to the new club at Harlech. It was of florid and fanciful design so More sent it to a Birmingham Goldsmith to be melted down and made into a solid Goblet. This in due course became the St. David's Gold Cup. Further important financial help came from Osmond (later Sir Osmond) Williams, Lord Lieutenant of the County, from Lord Harlech, Lady Amherst and Mrs. Holland, wife of Samuel Holland. Eventually, by diligent searching and persuasive argument More obtained a dozen members, each of whom contributed the obligatory guinea.

An aged Green Keeper was employed and, as an impressive badge of office, was given a scarlet tail-coat by a member who had given up hunting. Unfortunately, he, the Green Keeper, took to the bottle and in the words of More himself, 'His scarlet figure often became an entirely visible bunker, recumbent on the course. So much so that it was suggested that a ball lying near him might be lifted a club's length away, but not nearer the hole, without penalty!'

The first Treasurer was another old gentleman, a churchwarden and an unlikely drunkard; his confusion was, on one occasion, to put the collection into the club box! The first stewardess was a Mrs. Hughes, remembered as an attractive dark-haired woman. Her kitchen at the club, small as it was, became a popular informal

Royal St. David's Golf Club, 1908.

Dudley Maidment collection

meeting place where members often met, perhaps to dry themselves after a damp session on the links or just to chat. There was a story of a local rector seen sitting in the kitchen, sipping tea, fully dressed except for his trousers, while Mrs. H. was busy mending a large hole in the nether regions!

In a hurricane of rain and wind and in the presence of several famous golfers the club was officially opened on 2nd November 1894. W. Lowson, a genial Scotsman, was the first Captain, and the President was Harold Finch-Hatton himself, ten years later to be succeeded by his brother, the 13th Earl of Winchilsea.

There is little doubt, however, that it was William More himself who was the corner-stone of the club. Its Secretary for a total of thirty-four years, 1894 to 1921 and 1924 to 1931, he was a first class administrator, with an extraordinary gift for organising and running big tournaments. He was immensely popular with players and visitors alike and it was largely due to his efforts that local newspaper reports as early as 1902 were claiming that 'the links now take rank with the best in the United Kingdom and the increasing popularity of Harlech as a golfing resort places the little town in the forefront of West Wales

46

holiday haunts.' By 1903: 'Harlech is rising in popularity each year owing to the attraction of the Royal St. David's Golf Club which is in a most flourishing condition under the able management of its energetic and genial Hon. Sec., Mr. W. H. More.' The following year: 'Mr. More is in the truest sense an ideal secretary. It is difficult to associate the club without Mr. More, for it is in very large measure due to his efforts that Harlech has come to be recognised as one of the leading golf institutions in the country.' And the following year, 1905: 'If ever a golf club was fortunate in its secretary that club is the Royal St. David's.' By this time, too, the lists of those playing at Harlech read like something from *Debretts* or *Burke's Peerage*: Earl Winchilsea, Earl Amherst, Grand Duke Michael of Russia, Lord

Mr. W. H. More (with pipe), Mrs. More (behind her husband) and other members of his family and guests outside the Royal St. David's clubhouse.

Mrs. Pamela Proctor's collection

Lord Maidstone driving, 1907.

Dudley Maidment collection

Dargan, Sir Bryan and Lady Leighton, Lady Muriel Paget, Lady Cowley, Lord Southwell, Lady Holderness.

The impact on the town was significant also. Nearly all the Harlech children went caddying, sometimes for pocket money, but more usually to help family income. For the five-mile course there was normally a threepenny tip. 'But sometimes,' says Elsie, 'you didn't get anything at all if the ball was lost. We used to watch those balls with eagle eyes!'

Half way around there was a farm, Cefn Mine, with a small hut from which soft drinks and snacks were sold—ginger beer, milk and biscuits and so on. Most golfers would buy a drink for their caddies, but not much was thought of those who didn't treat and everything possible was done to avoid them during subsequent rounds. 'I remember caddying for Lord Alverstone,' says Elsie, 'then Lord Chief Justice of England. He had been trying the Crippen murder

48

case and he had come to Harlech to rest after the publicity surrounding the trial. He was absolutely charming and he called me his "sweet little caddy". He used to give me 1/6d a day, a princely sum. If I lost a ball he never grumbled, and on good rounds he used to hold me on high and say, "You've been a good little caddy today." His daughter used to start the rounds with him but she used to leave him after the first few holes, telling him to carry on, but not to go too far and to take it easy. Thereafter he would go by himself, with me as company. More often than not he would leave on the sixteenth green, the nearest to home, and go straight to his hotel. But he always stopped at Cefn Mine to make sure that I had a glass of ginger beer.

Lady Alice Amherst practising her swing, c.1908.

'Two other regular golfers were the Misses Holcroft,' continues Elsie, 'or they might even have been mother and daughter. They were both very bonny and attractive, and it was a treat to watch them. They had real style. One always wore a scarf tied around her hips and the loose ends would fly in the breeze. Both wore hobble skirts with buttons down the front. We used to love to imitate them, playing with sticks and with cotton reels for balls. We would tie something tight around our bottoms and wiggle them, just like the Holcrofts.'

'A well-known local caddy was Jack "Zebra",' says Laura, 'so-called because he never washed and had a perpetual tide-mark around his neck. He was a plain boy but he was a good caddy and popular with the golfers, especially at tournament time. One day, I was caddying for one gentleman and Jack was caddying for his partner. As always we caddies went in front while the golfers prepared to tee-off. At one green a large sandhill needed to be cleared and we stationed ourselves to watch the flight of the ball. When my player struck the ball it swung into the sun and I lost sight of it as it landed. I knew then that my threepence was in grave danger! I asked Jack had he seen it. He replied that he had but would only tell me if I kissed him. I replied that I would do no such thing and that I would rather do without my threepenny piece. With that he made a grab for me and there followed a frantic struggle, but rescue came when the two golfers suddenly appeared over the sandhill.

"What were you trying to do, boy?" asked one. Jack looked sulky.

"He was trying to kiss me," I said, "and I didn't want to."

He smiled. "I don't blame you, my dear," he said.

We never did find the ball, though I still got my threepence!'

'A caddy with a lot of style was Huw "Tan Llech"*,' continues Laura. 'He wore white plus-fours and, like Jack, was a popular caddy. He always caddied for the Prince of Wales when he golfed at Harlech. Sadly, Huw died of pneumonia while still quite young, but there was a touching sequel when the Prince sent money to buy a wreath.'

Captain of the club in 1914 was H. R. Stokoe. Stokoe was one of those stalwarts of golf, a good player, no more, occasionally having outstanding days, but whose enthusiasm and example influenced all

*The part of town where he lived.

50

Local children caddying, *c.*1907.

Dudley Maidment collection

those around him. A housemaster at Tonbridge School from 1890 to 1931 he played regular golf, cycling fifteen miles two or three times a week to his local club at Crowborough and back again. He came to Harlech nearly every holiday, just to play golf. He had two sons, both fine golfers in their own right. The older, Henry Bertram Stokoe, captained Oxford University golf in 1914. At Easter that year he carried all before him at Royal St. David's. He won the scratch handicap Gold Medal, the Easter Cup and Vice Captain's Cup and with his father he won the foursomes match play. It was said of him that he drove a long ball with such power that it would take him to the forefront of golf. Members of the club, proud that he had learned much of his golf at Harlech, were eagerly anticipating a golden future.

Sadly, Henry Stokoe, a Captain in the King's Own Yorkshire Light Infantry, was killed in action at Ypres in October 1915, aged twenty-one.

CHAPTER 7

Church and Chapel

On Sundays most children weren't allowed on the beach or do anything that would disturb the Sabbath or spoil their Sunday clothes.
They were allowed to read, but it had to be something 'proper'. They
were not allowed to whistle, or sing 'comic' songs.

'I remember singing a few bars of "Goodbyee" when it first came
out,' says Elsie, 'and I was sternly reprimanded by mother. "Don't
you dare sing such songs on a Sunday." Nevertheless, we always
enjoyed our Sundays. When we came home from Sunday School, tea
would be waiting, with the table beautifully laid. There would be
scones, perhaps a tart, jelly, and the best china set out, always.
Mother would wear her best clothes. I can see her now, sitting by the
fire, with all the brasses sparkling. She looked most regal, perhaps in a
black voile skirt (again, a gift from the Winchilseas) with flounces of
satin and a mauve blouse tied at the neck, and her hair just-so.'

Of the many places of worship in Harlech—St. Tanwg's Church
and the Baptist, Scotch Baptist, Calvinist, Wesleyan and Independent chapels—the biggest was the Welsh Baptist chapel, 'Tabernacl'.
The Baptists were very proud that 'Tabernacl' was the biggest and
the grandest. There was invariably a packed congregation, and the
singing was always powerful. It was a happy chapel. The Minister,
the Reverend David Davies, was a gentle and kindly man and, like
many ministers, a writer of poetry. Unlike some others, however, he
was always quietly spoken and did not possess that quality of
emotional, almost theatrical preaching so beloved of the Welsh, the
famous *'hwyl'*. Never well-paid, he nevertheless lived well. This was
because he was largely kept in food by the local farmers. Cynics often
used to claim that clerics only made their house-calls at meal times,
but David Davies was always a welcome visitor and was greeted with
great warmth whenever he called.

The position of the chapel elders, or deacons, was all-powerful.
There were six or seven in the Baptist chapel and they sat in the *sêt
fawr* a raised pew just beneath the pulpit. They chose the minister,
invited visiting preachers and decided chapel policy. At prayer meet-

Tabernacl Baptist chapel.

ings they would take the service, reading from the Bible and taking turns at praying. 'At such times we children would enliven the proceedings by noting little verbal idiosyncracies,' says Elsie, 'counting "humphs" or the number of times a phrase was repeated. One deacon we were particularly fond of was Francis Williams, a local farmer. We liked him partly because his prayers were short and sweet and partly because he was always late for chapel, his arrival being announced by the squeak of his boots. We would grin and nudge each other as we watched his stately progress, somewhat spoilt by squeaky boots, all the way down the aisle to the front of the chapel!

'We had a charming Sunday School teacher, Annie "Gwyndy", who had great patience with us,' continues Elsie, 'for we weren't really very religious. She vowed that as we were so naughty she would give up and pass us to one of the chapel deacons. This we certainly didn't want, because most of them seemed so strict, so we would be on

53

extra special behaviour for a week or two. Another greatly loved Sunday School teacher was Mrs. Richards. Her husband was a sea captain. He would be away for two or three years and when he came home she would invite us to her house, three or four at a time, for Sunday tea.

'Captain Richards was the most jolly of men. He had a concertina and he used to dance lively jigs to merry little tunes and sing songs that had more than just a flavour of the South Seas about them:

> O, wee wee a wa wakka.
> O, wee wee a wa wakka.
> Ani kooki ka
> So-on i metra
> Mam res, mam res
> Sani booli baya
> Mam amam oma
> Flimp an flo
> Flimp an flo
> Sami booli ba—aya.

Then more quickly:

> Pim strim stramadami
> Anabooni ring tin
> Arink na booli man a koi mi
> Koi mi nero
> Kelt i kero
> Koi me nero, koi mi
> Pim strim stramadami
> Anabooni ring tin
> Arink na booli man a koi mi.

'I'm amazed that I can remember these songs because I was very young then,' says Elsie. 'The words and melodies certainly weren't negroid—more Polynesian, as I've said. Captain Richards would sing and dance all the time we were there. We always looked forward to his homecoming and we would always come away with a penny or two.'

Tuesday evenings were Band of Hope evenings. They were held in the chapel vestry and a large number of children attended, perhaps fifty or sixty. They were looked forward to, because, like all children, they would giggle over different things. The Reverend David Davies would be there and he would teach Tonic Sol-Fa. They would learn a verse or two from the Bible but it was never a rigid or stilted religious affair. It was a happy event. They sang hymns, practised for the Singing Festival and were told little stories, 'Perhaps one or two from my uncle who was a deacon and who always had a fund of stories to make us laugh,' says Elsie.

Each March, when the winter season of evening meetings was over, there was a Band of Hope Festival. Baptist children would get the day off from school, there would be three o'clock tea and a concert in the evening, with recitations, dramatic performances and singing. For these events their mother taught the three girls a number of English songs:

Where is the land of I-don't-know-where?
Sleep is the driver to take you there.
Climb on his cart,
And away we'll start,
He won't charge much for the fare.
Where is the land of I-don't-know-where?
Don't be surprised at anything there.
The moon up on high,
Pigs that can fly,
Where? I don't know where.

★　　★　　★

There is a happy land
Far, far away,
Where three piggies play,
Three times a day.
Oh, see those piggies run,
When they see the butcher come.
Three slices off their bum,
Three times a day.

★　　★　　★

Down, down, down down down down,
Over the meadows, over the town,
This is the way that the snow-babies go
Eating their nighties of beautiful snow
Down, down, down down down down.

⭐   ⭐   ⭐

When good King Arthur ruled this land
He was a noble king.
He stole three pecks of barley meal
To make a bag pudding.

A bag pudding the Queen did make
And stuffed it well with plums
And in it put great lumps of fat
As big as my two thumbs.

The King and Queen
There oft did eat
And noble men beside
And what they could not eat at night
The Queen next morning fried.

These songs, all of which had charming melodies, were very popular with local audiences, partly because they were different from the Welsh songs normally sung.

'On one occasion,' says Elsie, 'mother taught Maria Owen and me a new song. All went well in front of an appreciative audience until, as Maria went into the last verse, I suddenly went back to the first. Eventually, as we realised that our words weren't matching, the whole thing fizzled out. We stood there on the stage, looking at each other, then we burst into a fit of giggles. Unluckily for me uncle was MC. He reprimanded us both quite sternly, saying that if we couldn't control ourselves then we ought to get off the stage. Suitably chastened we did, only for me to get a further telling off from mother when I got home. Now I *do* remember the last verse of that lovely song, "The Golden Shore", and it went something like this:

Now for ever, yes for ever
Those years have passed away
And now no more beside the shore
As children we shall play.
But this I know, in future years
When life's sweet dreams are o'er
That little maid and I will meet
Upon that golden shore.

'We always had new clothes for the concert,' says Beattie. 'We looked forward to this, of course. We had dresses from Lady Gladys and Mrs. More and mother used to cut them down to fit us. I remember an exquisite pinafore dress that was made for me in blue velvet, with Elsie having one in mauve and grey wool, both with pure white linen blouses. Our hair was beautifully done as ever. Despite our poverty mother always had us looking neat, crisp and clean. Our underclothes were white and all our petticoats had hand-crocheted frills, again done by mother. To this day I don't know how she did it all, or how she got the time. It seemed to be no trouble at all and it must have given her real pleasure. It was for this reason, no doubt, that mother was given dresses that wealthier families had no further use for, because it was obvious that so much use was made of them.'

The *Cymanfa Ganu*, or Singing Festival, was another great day in the Baptist calendar. Held on the first Monday in May, there were new clothes for this event, too, the start of summer attire. The Festival was held annually in different parts of the county—Harlech itself, Dolgellau, Bala, Tywyn, Barmouth—and each year excitement mounted with the approach of the great day. It would be even more exciting, of course, when the event was held outside Harlech, for it would involve a train journey, itself an experience, paid out of chapel funds. They would stand on the station platform in rows, boys behind the girls, to be counted before the tickets were booked. The children's service would be in the morning, when the best boy or girl would be given a special prize for Bible knowledge learnt during the preceding year. 'It was never our lot, of course!' says Elsie. In the afternoon it was the adults' service. The chapel would be packed with rows of mothers in the gallery with children in the pews down below. The singing was always excellent, especially at the evening service when the men would join in after their day's work, all the result of assiduous practice in the Band of Hope or on Sundays between five and six o'clock, before chapel. The Methodists, too, had a Singing Festival, but they never went away. The Baptists were the only ones who went to other towns, and this of course was a large part of the excitement. 'Children of other denominations were always jealous and were teased unmercifully about their bad luck!'

Always before their departure home there was a festive supper, prepared by the ladies of the host chapel. The children were fed first, adults later. There were mounds of sandwiches (with the ubiquitous tinned salmon the most frequent filling), cakes, *bara brith* (a fruit loaf), jellies and blancmanges. 'Then,' says Elsie, 'we would catch the last train home, happy and content, singing those lovely hymns and laughing all the way.'

Another great Baptist day was the summer picnic. Horses and carts, ponies and traps carried the cheerful families, with the last cart, more slowly, bringing up the rear with hampers of food. Up the steep tracks they would go, to reach a flat field suitable for games. The men would fetch water, build wood fires and boil the water in huge iron kettles, while the ladies unpacked the big two-handled wicker hampers, laying out the food on crisp white tablecloths spread out on the grass. 'We had the most wonderful picnics,' says Elsie, 'Scones, pies and cakes were eaten in vast quantities, there was hurdling, racing, and hide-and-seek. It never seemed to rain and it was always hot and sunny. And then, with evening drawing on, tired and grimy, we sang all the way home. But it wasn't hymns on that day!'

Elsie continues, 'In chapel we always sat in the same pew, alongside our aunt from Cae Du farm. She wore a black muff and she always had peppermints inside this muff. A terrible tease, she would put her hand inside as if to extract peppermints to hand around. We children would look expectantly, peeping perhaps between raised fingers as we knelt to pray. Out would come the hand from the muff, only to be holding, delicately, a white handkerchief. She would then gently dab the tip of her nose and put the handkerchief away again, rattling sweet papers inside the muff while she did so. Then she would relent, smile at us and pass these peppermint sweets, one by one, along the pew as we sat there patiently waiting. She also had a footstool, a particularly soft one. If we got into the pew first, before service, we used to try to use it ourselves, except that our legs just weren't long enough. When she arrived she would give us a long look and back along the row the stool would be shuffled.'

The most significant event in the Baptist calendar was, of course, the Baptism, when the chapel was always full. There was a large tank of water under the floor, and the floor boards were removed for the big occasion. Dressed in white, those to be baptised would descend the steps to be fully immersed, with the Minister wearing a black overall. 'I remember Laura being baptised,' says Elsie, 'and I sat in the front row of the gallery as I watched my sister go down the steps. Mr. Davies, our Minister, wasn't over-robust and as he tried to get hold of her by the neck to immerse her there seemed to be some sort of struggle and I started to cry because I thought he wasn't strong enough to hold her!' After baptism, children and adults were taken up the steps to four or five ladies of the congregation armed with large white towels who would dry them and take them to the vestry to get dressed.

'The normal age for baptism was fourteen, and when all my friends at school were being baptised I asked mother when it would be my turn,' says Elsie. 'Mother, however, said that I would have to wait until I was eighteen as Jack, my brother, and Laura had not been baptised until they were that age. Only with that maturity would I be able to know the full meaning of the ceremony. But I flounced away, very cross indeed, saying that I would leave the chapel and go to church instead. "You do as you wish," said mother, "but you will not be baptised at fourteen." So I left chapel and joined the church, for I just couldn't bear the thought of going to Sunday School and Sunday service with all my friends baptised and full members of the congregation, able to take part in Communion without me.

'Thus I became Church of England,' continues Elsie, 'going to the English services there with mother and Beattie, though I still occasionally went to chapel, partly to keep company with Cass, my friend. Unlike church, where the only learning required was the Creed, Collect and psalms, in chapel you had to get up frequently to say a

St. Tanwg's church.

60

verse. On one of my subsequent chapel visits I was asked to do this, but the only verse I could ever really put memory to was:

Iesu Grist, ddoe a heddiw,
Yr un un, ac yn dragywydd.
Jesus Christ, yesterday and today,
The same for ever.

'It was just my bad luck that uncle, once again, was in charge that Sunday, and he turned to me and said in Welsh, "Yes, and that will be the same one you'll have for ever too." I was very cross to be made to feel so embarrassed. I waited for him outside and when I saw him I said that I would *never* go to the Baptist Chapel again. And I never did.'

Elsie continues, 'St Tanwg's Church had a Girls' Friendly Society (GFS), which was held once a week in the vicarage. The vicar, the Reverend David Williams, had been a widower for some years, but his sister taught us to sew and knit and told us Bible stories. Then we would have a bowl of hot soup, even occasionally a box of sweets, followed by a little prayer from the vicar to send us on our way. He was a marvellous man, an excellent golfer, too, though he would often return after a day's golfing somewhat the worse for drink. But he was a popular man, with the people of Harlech as well as with the gentry, and he was sadly mourned on his early death at the age of forty-seven in 1915.

'The vicarage was, and still is, quite a long way from the village, and on dark nights we used to try to scare each other and say that there were ghosts about. Passing the gates of Crown Lodge was especially scary because the driveway through the trees appeared particularly dark. On we would scuttle, along the lonely road, never meeting a car, of course, rarely a bicycle, occasionally perhaps a man on horseback. It was all great fun, and we used to cuddle into each other if it was cold—and for comfort.'

One of the loveliest days of the year for Harlech children was Easter Sunday. During Easter week upper class English visitors came to open their Harlech homes before the summer season. On the Sunday they went to St. Tanwg's Church and, with there being only one service in English, at 11 o'clock, it was full. No doubt conscious of the

61

attention they created, they arrived in their broughams and landaus, from outlying villages as well as from Harlech, with postillions in their colourful uniforms causing an even greater stir of interest.

'Mother, too, would be at the service,' says Elsie, 'so Beattie and I had to see to Sunday lunch. Mother would put the meat in the oven, by the fire, and when I got home from chapel at 11 o'clock (in my chapel days) my job was to see to the potatoes and vegetables. Then we would rush out in order to be outside the church with our friends by half past twelve, all sitting in a long line on the low wall opposite the church to see the "parade". What a sight it was! The ladies wore the most magnificent and colourful creations, ostrich feathers in their hats, feather boas over their shoulders, veils over their faces, parasols of all kinds.' For weeks afterwards the children would mimic this at play. They, too, would swirl their non-existent trains and twirl their imaginary parasols, copying the fashions they saw displayed on Easter Sunday mornings.

CHAPTER 8

The English in Harlech

'Ah,' says Elsie, 'wonderful memories of beautiful ladies with slim waists and Dolly Varden hats. They all seemed to wear Dolly Varden hats, lovely wide-brimmed creations in straw, trimmed with ribbons or flowers, made popular by Charles Dickens' Dolly in "Barnaby Rudge". It was a fashion that swept society in the last years of the nineteenth century and was still to be seen in the first decade of the new century.'

In Harlech it was the Sunday morning service, especially at Easter, that was the prime setting for a dazzling display of fashion that each year set local mouths agape. On these Easter Sundays it was the children, themselves exquisitely dressed, who would come out of church first, usually accompanied by nannies. Parents then followed more sedately, but obviously very conscious of the effect they were creating with the onlookers. The kaleidoscope of colours, of primrose, mauve, pink and hyacinth blue, and the richness of chiffon, voile, muslin and lace would certainly cause gasps of admiration, and the contrast with local dresses of wool and cotton in sombre black and grey would be very marked. To the children of Harlech it was all pure delight, and in the imitative games that inevitably followed young girls would put tissue paper under their skirts to copy the swish and rustle of silk or taffeta.

Daily visitors also came, usually from Barmouth, in coaches pulled by anything up to six horses. Postillions would trumpet their imminent arrival and the children of the town gathered at the roadside as passengers threw down coins, invariably causing a mad scramble.

Each Saturday in the summer the town band was on parade, playing the tunes of the day in order to collect money for band funds, while on Sunday evenings after dinner, visitors elegant in evening dress would stroll as far as Pen Graig to listen to the young men of Harlech as they sang in informal concert. 'We ourselves, as children, would also love to go there on such evenings,' says Elsie, 'and sit on the grass to listen to those lovely, yet untutored voices.' But these were simple

THE

FINEST MUSICAL TREAT IN WALES.

HARLECH CASTLE

Musical Festival

Thursday, June 23rd, 1927, at 10, 2 & 6

'MOUNT OF OLIVES' | 'STABAT MATER'
(Beethoven)   (Rossini)

FIFTEEN CHOIRS 1,500 VOICES

FULL ORCHESTRA—leader Mr. Akeroyd

Presidents—J. M. HOWELL, Esq. and F. C. MINOPRIO, Esq.

Conductor-DR. HOPKIN EVANS.

Artistes—

Miss Mair Jones.   Miss Blodwen Hughes.

Mr. Walter Glynne.   Owen Bryngwyn

Miss NELLIE ROBERTS and Miss MAY ROWLANDS.

Accompanists—Madame DAVIES HUMPHREYS, A.R.C.M., & Mr. TOM JENKINS, Mus.B.

Morning and Afternoon—Hymn-Tunes and Choruses by the United Choirs, Selections by Single Choirs, Solos, and Orchestral Works.

Evening—"MOUNT OF OLIVES" and "STABAT MATER" Massed Choirs and Orchestra.

Admission (including tax) DAY Reserved Seats £1 2s. 6d. ; Second 12s.; Un-reserved 8s. 6d. Reserved Seats for any Single Meeting 8s. 6d.

MORNING or AFTERNOON, First 4s. 3d.; Second 3s.; Third 1s. 10d.

EVENING, First 5s. 9d.; Second 3s. 6d.; Third 2s. 4d.

Early Bookings for Reserved Seats earnestly requested. Hymn Tunes and Words, 4d.; Mount of Olives, 6d. O.N. 1s.; Stabat Mater, 1s. O.N. 1s. 6d.; Programme and Book of Words, 4d.

Apply to W. MORRIS JONES, Portmadoc, Hon. Sec.

Cheap Bookings and Special Trains and Buses from all parts, see Bills.

---

16   Edward Williams, Printer, Dolgelley

offerings. Most visitors came to attend the more formal entertainment of the annual Music Festivals, first organised as Temperance Concerts in 1867, the main sponsor being Samuel Holland. The concerts were held in the castle grounds each summer, and by the early years of the new century there were massed choirs of up to 1,500 voices singing under the direction of famous conductors such as Henry Wood, Edward Elgar and Walford Davies. People came from all over England to listen to these concerts, and the platforms of Harlech Station, itself opened in 1867, were extended largely to take the new passengers brought in by special trains.

But there were precious few facilities in the town to cater for these new visitors. Although the Castle Hotel was opened in 1876 and the Queen's already existed as a railway hotel, there were no restaurants or cafes. Many residents, however, quick to take advantage of the situation, supplemented their meagre income by selling alfresco afternoon and high teas, served on long trestle tables. There are many still living who remember the good-natured crowds thronging the streets and the festive atmosphere of these occasions. Unfortunately, however, a succession of wet summers caused a decline in attendance, and there are other memories of constant mud, of torrential rain and of expensive marquees collapsing under the sheer weight of water. The festival, sadly, was eventually discontinued in the early 1930s.

More permanent attractions proved to be the excellent golf and the fine setting of the town itself, built as it was around the magnificent castle, with safe bathing below and good walking in the hills and mountains behind. Such was the increase in the English population of Harlech, resident as well as temporary, that churchmen on holiday used to help by voluntarily taking English services at St. Tanwg's Church. Dr. Field, one of the great Victorian headmasters (at King's School, Canterbury) and by then Warden of Radley College, was a regular preacher to packed congregations there. A lover of all things Welsh, he eventually bought a house in the town and learned enough of the language to take Welsh services also.

Visitors were accommodated mostly in the larger houses and tended to board themselves. This meant that they bought their own food which was cooked for them by the landlady, an odd custom which created enormous difficulties in the kitchen, when timings for beef or lamb or chicken, together with different puddings, had to be co-ordinated to meet different eating times, with those who paid more sitting in the front parlour and those who paid less in the back.

'One regular visitor to my aunt's house, Clogwyn Villa, was a Dr. Bolus,' says Elsie. 'Year in, year out, he would come with his wife, two children, an adopted black daughter and a nanny. They were a charming family, always "front parlour guests" and were especially welcome visitors because they'd brought with them a go-cart, kept permanently at the house, and which was regularly used by us during the winter!'

In those days Lord and Lady Winchilsea had two homes in the town, the Plas (the Mansion), now a restaurant and Bron-y-Graig, sadly demolished in the mid-sixties. The Plas—a well-known coaching inn in the early nineteenth century known as 'The Blue Lion' and, before that, part of the Harlech estates of the Vaughans of Nannau—was bought in due course by a Mr. Hatton Wood. He left it in 1891 to his nephew Harold Heneage Finch-Hatton, along with considerable other local property. Finch-Hatton was the younger brother of the Earl of Winchilsea and the first President of the Golf Club. Now, owning so much property in the area, he began to live much of his time in Harlech, becoming High Sheriff of Merionethshire in 1903. The property passed to his elder brother, the 13th Earl, when he, Harold, died in May 1904 at the age of forty-eight, collapsing on the doorstep of his London house, 110 Piccadilly, after a morning run in Hyde Park. The Plas today is still an elegant building, with glorious views from its verandah and terraced gardens of the full sweep of Cardigan Bay below. Often called 'The Lord's House' during the Winchilsea era, it had four main bedrooms and four single, six servants' rooms, a dining room, a beautiful drawing room with two arched portieres, a gun room and a lofty timbered billiard room.

A pathway through the woods connected the Plas with the Winchilseas' other property, Bron-y-Graig. This house was surrounded by gardens with magnificent displays of azaleas and rhododendrons, many of which still remain, despite the disappearance of the house itself. The rose garden was especially attractive. There were wild cliff gardens, tennis lawns, badminton courts, undulating pasture and

66

Bron-y-Graig.

Dudley Balch collection

The Gardens of Bron-y-Graig.

Dudley Balch collection

67

water courses, with sheltered woodland paths suddenly giving way to spectacular panoramic views. Mr. Dudley Balch, one of seven gardeners there under Mr. Rice, the head gardener, and who now lives in retirement in Harlech, still remembers those lovely gardens with pride.

Henry Stormont Finch-Hatton was the 13th Earl of Winchilsea and the 8th Earl of Nottingham, a descendant of Sir Christopher Hatton, Queen Elizabeth I's Chancellor. The family home for three hundred years had been Kirby Hall in Northamptonshire, a fine Elizabethan house now in sad disrepair, but by the early years of the new century they had moved to Haverholme Priory, near Sleaford in Lincolnshire. There is little doubt, however, that the Earl and Countess loved their two new homes in Harlech.

The Earl of Winchilsea was a rather austere, even melancholy man, but the Countess, Anne, daughter of Admiral of the Fleet Sir Henry Codrington, was quite the opposite. With waist-long titian hair, high cheekbones and dark eyes she possessed an unusual beauty. But she is remembered mostly for her loving, unselfish nature. Ellen Terry, a life-long friend, said that when 'Nan' (her preferred name) came into the room it was as if the sun came out. She was witty, creative and energetic. She was musical, playing the organ at St. Tanwg's Church, and possessed a delightful soprano voice. She loved composing, her piano-playing was of concert standard, she painted competently and she was a pioneer of portrait photography.

At Christmas the Winchilseas hosted concerts for the local gentry. 'Lady Winchilsea's choir', as it was called, gave regular performances and a highlight of the winter season was a supper concert of Christmas music given in the candle-lit drawing room. 'Mother and I were members of this small but lovely choir,' says Laura, 'with Lady Winchilsea accompanying us on the grand piano. I remembered the songs that I learned from Lady Winchilsea all the days of my life as I sang in later years in choir and solo.'

The Winchilseas' eldest child was Gladys, a shy, sensitive, reserved girl although, like her mother, sweet-natured and good-humoured. She much preferred her nickname 'Topsy' for she never liked her own names, Gladys Margaret. These were chosen by her godparents, for her parents hadn't thought of a name for her, even at the christening.

68

Lady Gladys Winchilsea ('Topsy'), 1904. Photograph taken by the Countess of Winchilsea.

Sir M. Osmond Williams' collection

Sir Osmond Williams, taken some years before the war, in cavalry uniform.

Sir M. Osmond Williams' collection

Sadly, few men visited the Winchilsea household who were of an age, or were suitable partners for Topsy. Many were golfing companions of Lord Winchilsea. One of these, however, always a welcome guest, was Osmond ('Ossie') Williams, a friend of Topsy's two younger brothers. Osmond was the son of the first Baronet at Deudraeth Castle, some nine miles away, and grandson of the first Liberal MP for Merionethshire, a county which up to then had always returned Tories. Ossie was tall and good looking with blue eyes and dark hair. He used to walk the nine miles to visit them where he joined the family activities, going to church, playing parlour games, shooting and skating. But a crisis developed in the family as Topsy and Ossie fell in love. Disapproval of the match was expressed on political and social grounds, with the Earl criticising the Williams family as middle-class, Welsh country squires. Topsy, however, defied her family by becoming engaged to Ossie, although he left for South America shortly after and stayed there for many years. Eventually, in February 1912, they married, although neither set of parents attended the wedding. In 1913 Ossie went abroad again, this time leaving for Mexico, and Topsy went to Deudraeth Castle to await the birth of their first child. Shortly after he returned from Mexico the Great War broke out and Ossie rejoined his old Cavalry regiment, then transferring to the Welsh Guards when that regiment was formed in 1915. Sadly, he was killed in the September, leaving by then a son and also a one-month old daughter whom he had never seen. 'Lady Gladys's distress I recall well,' says Elsie, 'for there was no doubt that she loved him deeply. She never re-married, and devoted herself to bringing up her two children.'

The elder of Topsy's brothers, and the heir, was Guy Montagu George, Lord Maidstone, 'Toby' to both family and friends. He was a courteous and kindly boy although perhaps lacking the glamour of his younger brother. 'I remember the marvellous celebrations the family had when Toby came of age in May 1906,' says Elsie, 'culminating in fireworks and a huge bonfire in the evening with a barrel of tar being burned on Pen-craig.' In 1910 Toby married Margarette Drexel, the beautiful daughter of a wealthy American banker. This was a marriage welcomed by the Winchilseas for it meant an injection of American wealth into an impoverished English family. The wedding

71

took place in London, although much of the courtship had taken place at the Plas.

Lady Gladys Winchilsea.

Sir M. Osmond Williams' collection

Sir Osmond Williams, cradling his infant son, 1914.

Sir M. Osmond Williams' collection

73

Denys George Finch-Hatton, born in London in April 1887, was the third and last child. One of the most outstanding young men ever produced by Eton, he was an athlete of astonishing ability, a brilliant scholar, a good musician, a witty conversationalist and a fine actor. Debonair, amusing and charming with all around him, his immense popularity never caused malice or jealousy, certainly not in Guy who was so over-shadowed by his younger brother. In fact, they got on extremely well and were devoted to each other. 'I recall the fun they created,' says Laura, 'when they sang comic songs in duet at the local school during the summer of 1906 in aid of a fund for a new church organ.'

'I remember Denys so well,' says Elsie. 'He was tall, extremely handsome, witty and affectionate. He was loved by all in Harlech, especially the children, for he would always stop and talk to them. He used to come into the kitchen at the Plas to amuse the staff, often picking mother up in his arms and teasing her unmercifully. Eventually he emigrated to East Africa where he had an exciting and adventurous life, so wonderfully chronicled in Karen Blixen's book and in the film *Out of Africa*. To many he was the original "Great White Hunter", but sadly he was killed in a plane crash in 1931 and I remember the day the news came through, for mother broke her heart.'

Olwen Owen, now over ninety, lived as a young girl in Harlech at the time. In a family of ten children she and her brothers and sisters used to watch the Winchilseas from the small garden of their house in Tryfar Terrace which gave a view on to the Winchilsea gardens, peeping as the Earl and Countess and their children had tea on the lawn. Seeing them the Countess would smile and frequently ask a footman or maid to take over chocolates, cakes and fruit. 'We had a beautiful upbringing,' says Olwen, 'if only by watching that lovely Winchilsea family.'

The Winchilseas left Harlech in 1912. High living by the 13th Earl had depleted the family fortunes and they were forced to sell all their Harlech properties. On 30th August that year a large auction sold both major houses, and others too—Noddfa and Bron Heulog, shops, cottages, farms such as Cefn Mine, Brwynllynnau and Pant Mawr. In all, some 347 acres of Winchilsea property came under the hammer.

74

Three miles from Harlech at Glyn lived Lord and Lady Harlech, although most of their time was spent on their Shropshire estate. The family trace their connection back to the Princes of Powys and are descended from those Lancastrian defenders of Harlech castle during the Wars of the Roses. William Gore, who had been MP for Caernarfon Borough, married in 1815 Mary Jane, daughter and heiress of Owen Ormsby from Anglesey, whose name he assumed to become Ormsby-Gore. His son was also MP for Caernarfon and he, after a lifetime spent in public service as well as being a Groom-in-Waiting in the Royal Household, was created the first Baron Harlech in 1876. A popular local landowner, his elevation to the peerage was greeted with great enthusiasm by the people of Harlech who were no doubt proud that the name had been chosen for the title.

'I remember the third Baron well,' says Elsie. 'He was a lovely character, thickset and with a flowing beard, though he was only in his mid-fifties. He always came into town on a tricycle, dressed in a Norfolk jacket and with a check cloth cap, greeting passers by warmly as he went along. We were given a half-day from school when he and Lord Winchilsea laid foundation stones for the new Council Offices and Library on 27th May 1908. We were all lined up in our Sunday clothes to clap when they arrived.'

Half a mile outside the town at Plas Amherst lived Lord and Lady Amherst, in what is now a residential home for the elderly. There were connections with the Vaughans who, for centuries, owned much of the land in the area, as well as with General Sir Jeffrey Amherst, the first Baron, who was Commander-in-Chief of the British Army in North America, fighting the French in the Seven Years War. His son, the first Earl, when Ambassador to China in the early nineteenth century, refused to perform the Ceremony of 'Ko-Tou' to the Celestial Occupant of the Dragon Throne, thus helping to give a new word to the English language ('kow-tow').

The family home was Crosswood, near Aberystwyth, but the fourth Earl wanted to build another house in Harlech. Begun in 1906, Plas Amherst had a number of most unusual features: there was a four-poster bed in the smoking room, and the drawing room contained a large fireplace with decorative items from a Renaissance Italian bed as part of its surrounds. The gardens were breathtaking,

Plas Amherst, July 1907.

being full of sheltered and arcaded walkways and stretching down steep slopes to the shore below. The house took shape very quickly, with Lady Alice Amherst staying at the Castle Hotel during her frequent visits in order to supervise its progress. All was complete within the year and a Grand Housewarming took place in the summer of 1907, with large numbers of guests arriving in motorcades from Crosswood, Lord Amherst leading the way in his Benz. (Lord Amherst was the second man in Harlech to own a car; the first, perhaps surprisingly, was a butcher, William Owen.)

Frequent visitors to Plas Amherst were Lord Ludlow, the Earl of Plymouth, Lord Mostyn, Lady Cromartie, Lady Dolly Walpole, Lord Rodney, Sir Edmund and Lady Prys Pryse, Sir John and Lady Smiley, Lord Sanderson and Captain Roger Tempest.

The Amherst staff were always smartly attired. The maids' uniforms were particularly attractive; caps and cuffs were goffered (i.e. pleated with special irons) to crimp and flute the edges.

76

Four-poster bed in the smoking room, Plas Amherst.

Dudley Maidment collection

77

Lord Amherst, 1907.

Formal Amherst dinners were known for their long graces both before and after the meal, but Amherst parties and dances always had the reputation of being delightful affairs, although mystery surrounds two telegrams sent to the family after one such event. The first, to Lady Amherst, reads:

> Your wonderful kindness is great
> You conjure with fairies and fate
> You dance like a feather
> As spirits on heather
> But our train is awfully late.
>   Signed, The World, The Flesh and The Devil.

The second, to Lady Enid Vaughan, her daughter, reads:

> There is a young lady of Vaughan
> Who is merry from Dinner to Dawn
> Quite fearless of spills
> She rides on the hills
> So that all bless the day she was born.
>   Signed, Faith, Hope and Charity.

Lord Amherst died in 1910 at the age of seventy-four. Four years later, on 15th July 1914, his widow met Prince Jean Sapieha-Kodenski, a scion of one of Poland's most ancient and aristocratic families. It was a romantic meeting, in the Box of the Empire Theatre, Leicester Square. They fell in love and were married a few months later, 16th December, at Westminster Cathedral. They continued as frequent visitors to Plas Amherst, and both played a large part in organising events supporting the war effort: the indoor racquets court was turned into a hall for band practice and musketry training; in June 1915 she was one of the first to arrive on the scene after the enormous explosion at the Penrhyn Ammunition Works; in September of that year they organised a 'cigarette concert' for Welsh soldiers returned from the Dardanelles, with the Prince presiding and with songs by the Polish baritone Kurthoff; in December 1917 they helped to organise and were then guests of honour at a 'Theatrical Entertainment' for injured troops at the Aber Artro military hospital in Llanbedr. Thus the Amhersts, and the Prince and Princess

79

WERNFAWR HALL,

HARLECH,

On Saturday, September 4th.

A GRAND

'CIGARETTE' CONCERT

VOCAL AND INSTRUMENTAL

In aid of the Fund to supply comforts for the Welsh Troops at the Dardanelles.

The Polish Baritone

M. ROMEO KURTHOFF

HAS PROMISED TO SING.

Princesse Jean Sapieha

WILL PRESIDE.

Doors open at 8, Commence 8-30.

First Seats, 2/-   Second Seats, 1/-

Tickets may be had at the Post Office, Harlech, and at the Hall.

Printed by R. Isaac Jones & Son, Tremadoc.

Dudley Maidment collection

80

Prince Sapieha-Kodenski.

Dudley Maidment collection

Sapieha, no less than the Winchilseas, played a significant part in the social history of early twentieth century Harlech.

It was in 1897 that Alfred Perceval Graves, famous as the author of *Father O'Flynn*, and his wife Amy visited Harlech for the first time. On both sides, one Anglo-Irish, the other German, they came from old established families. They themselves had a large family and were obliged to rent two houses in Bronwen Terrace to accommodate them all for the duration of the summer. Perceval Graves has himself recorded that on a day when they were out blackberrying and gazing at the beautiful countryside around them Amy turned to him and said, 'I'd like to die here.' In response he had simply said, 'Why not live here first?' And so they bought land from John Lloyd, a local farmer, Amy paying his lawyer's fees as well as their own in order to speed negotiations. By the summer of 1899 all was finished and the first new house built in Harlech for many years was ready for occupation. All that remained was to find a name for it. With its fine westward aspect over Cardigan Bay and the Irish Sea they decided on the Welsh translation of 'towards Ireland'; thus Erinfa it became, as it still is today.

Perceval was a distinguished, kindly and courteous man. He would always stop and talk to the local children who responded enthusiastically to his warmth and 'Father Christmassy' white beard. Extremely devout, he always officiated at family prayers in which the servants were invariably included. Beryl Thomas, who now runs a restaurant and tea shop in the town, worked for the Graves family for thirteen years and her mother worked for them for thirty-two years before that. She recalls that the servants were required to attend the service every morning before the family breakfast. For years, too, every Sunday without fail he taught at the Church Sunday School, captivating the children with his soft Irish brogue. He played his part in a wider field also. He loved the Welsh language which he spoke quite well and he made a special study of Welsh poetic measures and folklore. In recognition of his contribution to Welsh life and culture he was enthroned as Bard at the National Eisteddfod in Blaenau Ffestiniog in 1898. He died in 1931 and lies buried under a simple Celtic cross in Harlech churchyard, with Amy, who died twenty years later, alongside him.

Amy herself came from an aristocratic German background which showed itself in her imperious bearing. She was Teutonic in every way, taller than her husband and altogether bigger-boned. Somewhat inelegant and seen always in a long black dress, she regularly carried with her a large and cumbersome carpet bag. She had a loud voice, heavily accented, and was once overheard to say at a concert where the pianist was playing with great bravura and no little skill, 'What a wonderful pianist. He must have been conceived in great passion.' A

The grave of Alfred Perceval Graves and Amy Graves, parents of Robert Graves.

fine worker for the church and local people, she was a generous philanthropist who brought home-made soup to all and sundry in all weathers, even when she herself was in her late eighties. In 1947 she had a splendid 90th birthday party at the Plas Restaurant, still remembered by many in the town today.

The outbreak of war in 1914 had placed Amy in an invidious position, especially with so much anti-German feeling, in Harlech as elsewhere in Britain, where German seamen in ports, German waiters, commercial travellers and shopkeepers were treated with great hostility. It was only the year before, in the summer of 1913, that Amy's cousin, General Friedhelm von Ranke, while staying with them, had reviewed the Harlech boy scouts and communicated to them a telegram from the Kaiser himself, blessing the movement. But her own fierce loyalty to the British Crown was never in question, and she was especially proud when her son Robert volunteered early in August 1914. It was at the Golf Club that the decision was reached for Robert to join the Royal Welch Fusiliers, and it was the Secretary, Mr. W. H. More, who suggested that regiment. When Mrs. Graves exclaimed what a pity it would be if Robert were to kill one of his German uncles, Mr. More laconically replied, 'My dear Mrs. Graves, it would be far worse if one of Robert's uncles killed him.'

Robert Graves himself loved Harlech deeply. Almost every leave he returned there from a war service so graphically recorded in *Goodbye to all that*. After the war he bought a two-roomed cottage from his mother, who by now owned considerable property in the town. He whitewashed it, furnished it simply and put in a big window to overlook the woods below, towards Morfa Harlech and the sea. But more than town, or castle or beach, he loved the wild desolate countryside behind. Here he gathered bilberries, blackberries; even pieces of Roman tiling. He and his brothers and sisters walked for hours over those hills and he said that he came to know that part of Wales more purely than perhaps anywhere else in the world, finding there a great personal peace.

One of the most beautiful women in Harlech was Mrs. Kathleen Isabelle Carter-Campbell, married to Arthur Carter-Campbell of Possil in Lanarkshire, a descendant of the Earls of Breadalbane and related by marriage to Mrs. Patrick Campbell. Always supremely

84

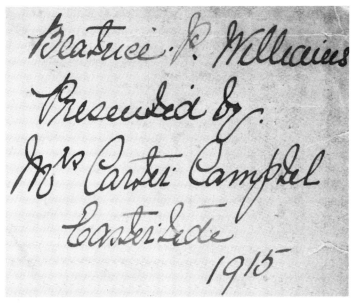

New Testament presentation page: Mrs. Carter-Campbell to Beatrice.

Author's collection

elegant, she dressed invariably in white, with suits and dresses cut to show off her superb figure to advantage. 'During the war,' says Elsie, 'many Harlech children were invited to go to her house to knit socks and comforts for Welsh soldiers. Beattie and I would go there together to make up parcels, and she would give us little extras to put in for our brother Jack on war service—needles and thread, cigarettes, paper and pens. Mother sewed for her, both at home and at her house in Bronwen Terrace, a large house where she lived all year except when she went to London for the Season. She was extremely generous and I remember the first Christmas of the war when she gave mother a magnificent food hamper.'

'She was a lovely person,' echoes Beattie, 'and she became my God-mother when I was christened at the late age of eleven. She was very aristocratic and came from an Italian background. I stood in awe of her. She would often call for me to attend morning service with her, but she always insisted that we sat upstairs in the small sunlit gallery.

The vicar at the time, the Reverend Robert Jones, a most sarcastic man, would ask before the sermon for the congregation to gather below and not to sit up in the gallery. I was highly embarrassed and really wanted to move down, but Mrs. Carter-Campbell had other ideas; she held me down tightly and despite repetition of the request we continued to stay "aloft".'

The Carter-Campbells were unhappily married. It was common knowledge that he drank too much while she became low spirited and downcast. The marriage ended in tragedy with her leaving him and with his suicide some time after. Their only son Lorne, who had fought as an officer in the war and survived, was killed in an accident on the Cresta Run in Switzerland in 1928.

'A rather strange resident was old Miss Walton,' says Elsie, 'reputedly a retired actress and who lived alone. She would be seen on the streets of the town with her wrinkled face covered in make-up, a red wig on her head and carrying a pekinese dog. She was supposed to be madly in love with old Dr. Jones, and it was said that she built an upper extension to her house just so that she could watch him while he worked in his garden at Pen-y-Garth, now the YHA, a little lower down from where she lived. Maria and I at first used to run errands for her, and she would give us pocket money. One day, however, we must have found her unprepared, for when she opened the door to our knock she was in her dressing gown and without her wig—standing there completely bald! We both turned tail and fled!'

Others who came to Harlech more or less regularly, either as independent holiday-makers or as house guests of the more permanent residents, were the Frys, the chocolate makers; the Birds family, then as now a household name; General George Carter-Campbell, who commanded the 51st Highland Division in the Great War, brother of the above-mentioned Arthur; the Oppenheimers; the van Straubenzees; George Bernard Shaw; George Mallory, who was to lose his life on Mount Everest; Siegfried Sassoon, who wrote *The Huntsman* in Graves' cottage; the novelists H. G. Wells, Richard Hughes, Hugh Walpole, who wrote *Fortitude* while staying in Harlech, and E. H. Benson; the Pilkingtons, glass manufacturers; Ellen Terry; Elspeth Huxley; the Webbs; Gerald du Maurier; Sir William Preese, pioneer of wireless telegraphy; the musicians Gustav Holst, Sir Granville

Bantock, Josef Holbrooke, Eugene Goosens and Cyril Scott; Charles Maude the actor; Clement Davies, the Liberal politician; a group of Oxford and Cambridge academics, Doctors Field, Farquharson and Murray, who came to play golf together in the Christmas meeting of 1911; Dr. James, Headmaster of Rugby; Dr. Fisher, Headmaster of Oundle; Max Beerbohm, who had a house locally; Augustus John; George Buckle, editor of *The Times*; Dr. Winnington Ingram, Bishop of London; Frank Woolley, the Surrey cricketer; Philip Morris RA; and the Prince of Wales himself, later Edward VIII, who played golf there as a young man and later became Captain of the club.

At Crown Lodge lived Mr. William Henry More, that popular Club Secretary mentioned at length in the chapter on Harlech Golf. Appointed Receiver for the Crown lands in North Wales and Monmouth, it was stipulated that he must therefore have a residence in Wales. Merionethshire was suggested as the county, the Crown having no Sub-Agent there and Harlech, formerly the county town, was proposed as being very suitable. So he came to Harlech in 1891, living at Noddfa while the official residence was built. Unhappy at

Christmas 1913 at Crown Lodge; Mr. and Mrs. More (centre middle) and family.

Mrs. Pamela Proctor's collection

first, for his wife wept at being brought to such a 'desolate place', they eventually lived there in great contentment for over forty years. He died in 1934 and lies buried in St. Tanwg's Church. Mrs. More was a lovely woman, 'just like Queen Alexandra', some recall, and an admired hostess at tennis parties and evening soirees. She herself was an accomplished pianist, always in great demand as an accompanyist at local concerts.

There were six children, three boys, of whom Jack and Frank fought in the First World War, and George, a Royal Air Force pilot, in the Second World War, and three girls, Constance, Evelyn and Peggy. They had a Welsh governess and it was an important part of her duties, on their father's instructions, to teach them Welsh. The eldest daughter Constance, who was married in 1913, had the first white wedding in Harlech, an event that naturally had to be commemorated in children's games for months afterwards. 'I was usually the blushing bride,' says Beattie, 'with mother's lace curtains on my head, parading up and down the street. My "husband" would be Cassin "Sam". Sam Williams, Cassin's father, the postman, would have his blue trousers with the smart red stripe purloined for the occasion.'

More's clerk for twenty-nine years, from 1891 to 1920, was Robert Owen, whose job it was, with More, to collect rents from the Crown lands in the area, as far south as the monastery of Strata Florida near Pontrhydfendigaid. The two always went by rail because of the excellent service of those days, with a train every two hours throughout the day and two on Sundays. Away overnight, they were regularly entertained at various rent audit dinners at local inns throughout North and mid-Wales, with huge meals being followed by rousing songs.

Mr. Owen was a man of remarkable punctuality. Many in Harlech swore they could set their watches from the time he walked down the street to post the official letters, carrying the imposing black bag with the Crown and Royal Cypher. This was always at 4.55 p.m. exactly, in order to catch the 5 o'clock post.

Owen's daughter, Bessie, still lives in Harlech and recalls that her father, although chronically asthmatic, belonged to the local defence volunteers. She remembers as a child toddling alongside him as he was marching, asking him if he was alright! Bessie still lives in the house where she was born, a house that was rented from the Graves family at £8 a year. With two rooms and kitchen downstairs and two rooms upstairs it was excellent value for money. The Crown lands have long since been sold off but there are mementoes of that era in Bessie's home, in the inscribed books that were given by Mr. and Mrs. More each Christmas and in the desk whose plaque shows that it was given by them as a wedding present to her parents on their marriage in 1901.

From left to right: Evelyn More, Jack More, Peggy More, Frank More, unknown.

Mrs. Pamela Proctor's collection

89

Jack More and Commander Lyne outside Crown Lodge, 1915.
(Commander Lyne was the son-in-law of Mr. More)

Bessie Owen, 1987.

Author's collection

In the summer of 1916 Alvin Langdon Coburn came to live in Harlech. Considered at that time to be the world's finest photographer he and his wife Edith, both Americans, Bostonians, were so charmed with Harlech that they bought a plot of land, 'Cae Besi' (Bessie's Field) and built a house there, later building another not far away so that their friends could come to stay. They lived in Harlech for nearly thirty years, loving the town, and Wales, very deeply. They, too, played their full part in Welsh life. Edith in the Second World War was Commandant of the Harlech Red Cross and ran a small hospital for evacuated children. Coburn himself, a perennial enthusiast and showman, threw himself energetically into a number of activities, especially those which involved dressing up. He became a Grand Officer in the Freemasons, he was a lay preacher in the Church of Wales and later proudly donned the green robes of an Ovate in the Welsh National Eisteddfod. They moved to Colwyn Bay in 1955, Edith dying shortly after, but Coburn living on until his quiet death there in 1966, a long way from Boston.

One of Harlech's most interesting residents was Mr. George Davison, school friend of William More, and the person who had been the first to introduce Alvin Coburn to Harlech. George Davison was an outstanding landscape photographer who had become co-Managing Director of Kodak (with George Eastman) in 1900. Although he was a very wealthy man, having obtained his money through careful buying of Kodak stock, he was a vociferous communist and once led a group of anarchists down London's Kingsway carrying a banner emblazoned 'Down with Capitalism'. He was also actively involved in militant socialism amongst the miners of South Wales. Owing to these and other activities he was asked to resign as Kodak's Managing Director, and in 1907 he retired to Harlech to devote himself to the welfare and education of the Welsh poor. Here he began to build a large and imposing house overlooking the golf course. The people of Harlech watched the building of this house with curious interest, especially as it gave work to so many local people. Built to an exceptionally high design standard, Wern Fawr was completed in two years, 1908-1910. It is now the home of Coleg Harlech.

George Davison's impact on Harlech was immediate and

Wern Fawr, built on the site of an old quarry.

considerable. To some the house became a hotbed of left-wing anarchy, to others a centre for intellectual debate (Shaw and the Fabians were frequent visitors), to yet more a centre for outlandish parties, with naked ballerinas from London performing on stage, or so local gossip claimed! A number of Harlech's residents, not unexpectedly, disapproved of his activities and of his atheism. Apparently he had been a religious man but said that he had seen so much poverty in London that he could not bring himself to believe that a just Being could allow such suffering.

George Davison was exceptionally generous. Every week during the winter months he would give groceries and coal to the widows and spinsters of Harlech, although nothing was ever given to church or chapel. 'Atheist he might be,' says Elsie, 'but mother always claimed that he was doing things the Almighty would approve of. He would walk the streets of the town hatless (unusual in those days), with sandals on his feet. We children loved him. Every Christmas he gave a children's party. There was always a huge tree, beautifully decorated, festooned with wonderful gifts. One of the gardeners with a high ladder had to get the topmost gifts down, and this the children would watch with bated breath lest he fall off the ladder or, worse still, bring the tree down.' The atmosphere was gay and exciting and Davison joined in the fun with great good humour. This was always followed by a Boxing Day Fancy Dress Ball with Davison as judge. Says Elsie, 'Mother, with Huw Jones the tailor and Mr. Walker the golf professional were always the three who would organise and run the event.' 'For one of the balls,' says Laura, 'I wore Lily Elsie's original "Merry Widow" gown. Lily Elsie used to stay at the Plas, and at this time the gown was stored there for the shows and events they used to hold. Nobody was staying there at the time and the caretaker, who was friendly with mother, took it out of store and lent it to me for the ball. It was a great risk for him, of course, but I hope it was worth it because I was told I looked just like the great Lily herself.'

There were regular musical events on summer Sundays, with piano recitals and concerts given for the benefit of local people. There was a magnificent pianola organ in the Great Hall and guest organists were brought from London to play. 'Many recitals were given by George Davison and Alvin Coburn,' says Elsie, 'with Davison playing the organ and Coburn the piano. Davison would sit quite erect but Coburn would play with great flourishes, swaying from side to side, eyes closed. Beattie and I would nudge each other as, somehow, his trousers used to work their way up his legs, revealing socks of the most violent patterns and hues. That was always the best part for us and we would try to guess, as we made our way there, what socks would be revealed that night!'

'In a competitive concert in the Great Hall,' says Laura, 'when I was fourteen, I performed a beautiful old Welsh ballad, ("*Ce's lythyr heddiw gan fy mam*"—A letter from my mother) which was well received by the audience. The adjudicator said I had a sweet voice with clear diction and feeling. He advised me to sing mezzo in order to preserve my voice and afterwards he suggested to mother that I should go for training. Poor mother, naturally, could never afford the payments for me to become a professional singer. It was my ambition to become a concert performer but it was not to be.'

'Mother, for many years both before and after she broke her leg, was a teacher of dancing at Mr. Davison's house,' says Beattie. 'Many in Harlech learned their first steps there under mother's tuition, though the more narrow-minded thought it terrible that dancing was taught at all.' But there are those who still recall the pleasure of taking their dancing slippers secretly to a weekday chapel meeting, and then running from there in gleeful anticipation to a dance class at Wern Fawr afterwards. 'Mother used to take me down as a young child,' continues Beattie, 'and I remember watching the sheer grace of those dances. At fourteen I was allowed to join in and it was a marvellous feeling.'

'Mother organised concerts, too,' says Laura, 'often writing the scripts herself as well as making the costumes. After one of these concerts Mr. Davison gave her one of his beautiful photographs. It was a study of the castle in the evening sun, with gathering storm clouds behind—but sadly the picture has long since gone.'

In the summer months parties of children and their teachers from the slums of London came to stay at Wern Fawr. Davison gave them regular holidays, pitching a large tent on the beach where the children could stay all day long to benefit from sun and sea air. In the evening he would give them magic lantern shows.

In the autumn he held discussion groups, 'or communist activities', as some accused. 'Regulars at these meetings were the headmaster Daniel Jones, many other leading lights and our chapel deacon uncle,' says Elsie. 'Auntie used to say to him on his return, *"Wyt ti wedi bod hefo'r tacla 'na eto?"* (Have you been with that lot again?). Uncle used to respond vehemently that George Davison was right in many of his views. Besides which the meetings were jolly enjoyable!' However, her resentment only reflected a wider resentment that was building up against George Davison. He eventually left Harlech in some disgust, but there were rumours also, probably well-founded, that he was under investigation from government security services who were questioning his financing a paper called *The Anarchist*. He was warned to leave the country and, in the early 1920s, he did so, buying the palatial chateau that King Leopold of Belgium had been building for himself at Antibes in the South of France. Here, in the 'Chateau des Enfants' he brought up any child provided its parents were prepared to renounce all rights to it. Communism and other left-wing views flourished, with George Davison presiding over the discussions, a dyspeptic, dressed always in a white suit, living almost entirely on a diet of nuts.

He died in 1930, a millionaire.

CHAPTER 9

Life in Service

As described by Laura:
'I left Harlech in 1910 when, at the age of fourteen, I became a between maid at Tan-yr-Allt (Under the hill). Built by William Madocks in the early years of the nineteenth century. It was an elegant two-storey villa with shallow roof, projecting eaves, innovative casement windows and a wide verandah supported by slim pillars, from which there was a splendid panorama of Traeth Mawr sands below. Now the home of the Snowdonia Rudolf Steiner School, it was a house of charm and simplicity which became a model for the new homes of wealthy land-owners throughout North Wales.

'In preparation for this great day, my first "situation", mother was sewing for weeks on end, making underwear, nightdresses, print frocks, aprons, then packing them all ready to go. I had been very lucky to get this appointment in that a friend of mother's had made the suggestion to Miss Greaves, the owner of Tan-yr-Allt, that I would be a suitable "tweenie". I joined a staff of chauffeur, two gardeners, cook, parlourmaid and housemaid.

Tan-yr-Allt, Tremadog.

'I was up at 5.30 each morning to clean and blacken the grates, light the fires in the kitchen and morning room, take hot water upstairs and help to prepare breakfasts downstairs. I was taught to set the servants' table—and servants were often stricter than those upstairs. Throughout the day there were pots and pans I had to scour until they gleamed, and at the end of the day I would wash the kitchen floor and scrub the huge kitchen tables. It was no wonder that my hands were red and raw and that I fell into bed exhausted each night!

'Miss Greaves, a member of the wealthy Greaves family that owned the Llechwedd quarries in Blaenau, was a wonderful employer. She insisted that I should be treated with the utmost kindness and given plenty of nourishment, saying that I was growing fast and looked anaemic. She may have been right, for I did seem to feel better, but this no doubt owed just as much to a happy life and kind people around me.

'In due course I became cook's helper. I was taught how to set a table for guests, to prepare sauces, how to make cream crackers. I learned how to prepare and cook complete meals, lunch or dinner, being encouraged always to build up my own recipe book. There is no doubt that I was most fortunate to be at Tan-yr-Allt. I was lucky, too, in that Miss Greaves was a generous hostess, buying only the best ingredients. Quarts of milk arrived daily, the farmer pouring it directly into a flat dish in the kitchen, and it rippled so thickly as we skimmed it that it could almost be used as cream itself.

'At lunch times there would be huge legs of mutton, or beef or game, with five or six varieties of vegetables arranged on silver platters. The smells were delicious as the house and parlour maids carried the dishes into the dining room—a daily ceremony. But Miss Greaves made sure that the staff, too, ate as well as she and her guests did.

'Miss Greaves was away a great deal, and went to Switzerland each Christmas, but she always instructed that we enjoy ourselves. This we certainly did and there was always laughter and fun.

'There was quite a beautiful garden at Tan-yr-Allt in which on June nights the ghost of Shelley was supposed to dance, Shelley having often stayed at the house as a young man, writing *Queen Mab* there.

97

He was reputed to have appeared naked in front of his house guests, but whether his ghost was equally unclothed we never found out!

'One summer night, when Mary the housemaid and I were walking arm in arm after supper, we did, indeed, see a ghostly figure in white just by the rose garden. Terrified, we clung to each other, then we flew towards the house. But the figure in white was quicker, running up the steps in front of us. Ghosts don't run, of course, and when we got indoors we found the chauffeur, grinning and almost as much out of breath as we were, with a white sheet, not quite well-hidden enough, peeping out from a cupboard in the hall!

'In Edwardian society the "At Home" afternoon was an important social event. Miss Greaves was at home once a month, and on that day Kate the cook would be working hard all morning, with my help. There would be fresh salmon and cucumber sandwiches, scones, jam and cream, iced fancies, meringues and a fruit cake, popularly known as a "cut and come again cake". It was always a wonderful event. During the afternoon carriages would arrive at regular intervals, and we used to love to watch the ladies (no gentlemen on these afternoons) as they walked on the lawns in all their finery, protected against the sun's glare (it always seemed to be sunny) by delicate parasols. On such occasions the coachmen had tea in the servants' hall where they ate huge mounds of food, as if they hadn't been fed for weeks. Certainly none seemed to eat as well as we did, and they all said they loved to come to Tan-yr-Allt.

'Miss Greaves was well known for her hospitality and kindness. She was a lovely person, and although she wasn't physically attractive, being tall and rather plain, perhaps even masculine, when she smiled her whole face became almost beautiful. Perhaps she knew this, for she smiled a lot. Her sunny disposition and gentleness never failed to bring happiness into people's lives. There was a young and lovely girl in the nearby village of Tremadoc. It was known that she had consumption, so Miss Greaves invited her three or four days a week for lunch. Each day she was brought in by Miss Greaves' carriage, and lunch was taken in the conservatory with flowers and plants all around. We kept her cutlery and crockery in disinfected water for her own use. She didn't live long, but Miss Greaves' kindness made her life happier, and maybe prolonged it a little also.

'The three years I spent at Tan-yr-Allt were amongst the happiest of my life, but in 1914, at the age of eighteen, I joined the Harlech household of Mrs. Carter-Campbell, a stunningly beautiful woman of Italian descent. There were six of us in service—parlourmaid, housemaid, lady's maid, pantry boy, a gardener and me, with my now having advanced sufficiently to be cook. The work was hard, for the staff were up each day at dawn, lighting fires for hot baths, and we were kept constantly busy until last thing at night.

'Although they were a wealthy family Mrs. Carter-Campbell was a most extravagant person and spent her husband's money quite lavishly. She was a moody person to work for, but very generous. During the war she organised classes to knit for soldiers, and mother became a regular help in the house because she could turn her hand to anything. Indeed, Mrs. Carter-Campbell and mother became so friendly that she, Mrs. Carter-Campbell, became Beattie's godmother when she was christened.

'Mrs. Carter-Campbell was very much in love with a handsome and charming young Army officer. Her personal maid swore that she used to drink scent to perfume her breath to be kissed. He was in Harlech on leave in the summer of 1915 and it was during that summer that Mrs. Carter-Campbell had large evening picnic parties on the beach. I would prepare hampers of boned chicken, whole hams, sherry cake, small home-made loaves and compote of fruit. There would be various salads and quarts of cream. These hampers were then carried down to the beach by the gardener and pantry boy and they used to come back and tell us girls tales of naked bathing which shocked our puritan minds, though certainly the behaviour of Mrs. Carter-Campbell and her young lover seemed to be indiscreet in the extreme.

'By the autumn, however, her young lover was in France with his Regiment. Not many months later the dreadful news reached Harlech of his death in Flanders. Mrs. Carter-Campbell was prostrate with grief. She was quite unconsolable. The following Sunday was Easter Sunday and Elsie, who was at the service, remembers vividly the congregation singing the Easter hymn:

On the Resurrection morning,
Soul and body meet again;

No more sorrow, no more weeping,
No more pain.

On that happy Easter morning
All the graves their dead restore;
Father, sister, child and mother,
Meet once more.

At that point Elsie told me that Mrs. Carter-Campbell sat down and sobbed and sobbed. Apparently it affected everybody; her terrible grief saddened the whole congregation and many were weeping along with her.

'A few days later she called me to her. She told me that she was going to London and leaving her husband. She said she would give me two months' wages, but that Mr. Carter-Campbell would be selling the house in the meanwhile. I never saw her again.

'Two weeks later Mr. Carter-Campbell, whom I rarely encountered, told the parlourmaid that he wished to see me. A little scared, I knocked on the door and entered. I stood, rather rigid as I recall, with my back to the door. First he thanked me for the mocha pudding I had made for lunch. Then he asked me to sit down on the couch. But I didn't move. He complimented me on my figure and told me how attractive I was. On my dignity I replied, "Is that all, sir?" But with that he strode over, caught my wrist, and pleaded with me to go away with him. I asked him who did he think I was. Out of loyalty both to my late mistress and to my own conscience I would never do such a thing. I flounced out of the door, forgetting to curtsey. The three girls were listening outside and I remember my mixed feeling of annoyance that they should have been eavesdropping and relief that they had been. He was quite possibly drunk, he very often was, and I felt low and degraded. I gave in my notice immediately, but I needn't have bothered for soon afterwards I was told that he himself was packing to go. Some months later we heard that he had committed suicide. It was a sad end to a very sad episode in my young life and in the life of Harlech.

'By the summer of 1916 the war seemed never-ending, with the whole town becoming increasingly sorrowful with the depressing

100

news from all fronts. But then, while I was home with mother, there came a letter from a Mrs. Higham of Southport, asking me would I care to join her household. Apparently my name had been given to her by a girl from Harlech who had recommended me as cook. My friend Merdeg also had been recommended as housemaid, for there was a vacancy here, too. We both accepted with delight and we duly arrived at Mr. and Mrs. Higham's imposing house in Southport or, more exactly, Birkdale, a wealthy dormitory town for Liverpool and Manchester.

'I liked Mrs. Higham from the start, and she me. The daughter of Sir William Hartley, famous then as now for his jams and preserves, she was charming, pleasant and kind. The only drawback was that she was somewhat mean with food—even the butter was locked up. Her husband was Liberal Member of Parliament for Sowerby, Yorkshire, and equally pleasant. They had three sons and a daughter and I was particularly fond of the youngest son Guy and his sister, Christine.

'Mrs. Margaret Lloyd George came to visit during the first week of December, and a magnificent dinner party was to be held in her honour. She stayed two nights and the party was on the night prior to her departure for London with Mr. and Mrs. Higham. On this night there was great excitement in the Southport household. The dining room was beautifully decorated by maids from Sir William Hartley's own staff and the tables looked exquisite with smilax and flowers everywhere. Twenty-eight people sat down to a very successful six-course dinner, ending with a fresh sponge cake layered with pineapple and *crème anglaise*, finished with fresh cream and topped with grated chocolate. It was rather extravagantly prepared for wartime but, after all, we were able to draw on Sir William's own lavishly stocked store rooms with his own preserves, lemon cheese, tins of fruit and jellies!

'The following morning the kitchen staff were given an unexpected honour with a visit from Mrs. Lloyd George herself, just before her departure. As I curtsied she pressed a gold sovereign into my hand and said how much she had enjoyed the meal.

"May I ask for the recipe for the sweet, my dear?" she asked.

'Much honoured, I naturally agreed, and added that it was my own recipe.

"Oh," she said. "And what is your name, my dear?"

"Laura," I replied.

"Would you permit me to call it 'Laura's Pudding'?"

I was so overwhelmed that I hardly remember how I replied, but I have often wondered if there is still a "Laura's Pudding" in the Lloyd George household.

'That was the day, too, that David Lloyd George became Prime Minister.'

CHAPTER 10

Farm Life

'The happiest days,' says Elsie, 'were those spent on uncle's farm, Cae Du (Black Field). It was a big farm, one of the largest dairy farms in the district, for uncle delivered milk to the big houses, the only farm to do so. I was very fond of Aunt and Uncle "Cae Du". Beattie and I were sent there for six months during the summer of 1911 after mother had broken her leg and was advised by the doctor to get away and spend some time with her sister in Liverpool.

'At first I hated the smell of the farm workers' sweat and the odour of animals on their bodies. Despite being a tomboy I was fastidious in many ways, and auntie used to get cross with me because as soon as the men came into the big kitchen for bread and buttermilk, the smell of which I hated equally, I used to go out into the yard. On the other hand Cae Du was great fun, because the farmhands used to tease us and play games with us, especially a farmhand named Johnny and Jack, our brother, both of whom worked there already.

'Auntie and uncle had adopted a young girl called Cassie, one of a family of six girls, all left orphans. Their parents had died of TB, rife in Harlech at the time. She and I used to play in the yard or go running through the long grass in the great fields high over the sea. Anything to get away from the kitchen!

'At night most of the men slept in the loft but Jack and Johnny slept in the room next to ours. A peculiarity of the dividing wall was that it did not reach the ceiling, hence there was a gap of a foot or so at the top. They would throw items of clothing or the odd boot over the partition to land on our bed, the resulting screams bringing auntie to our room to scold us.

'On one occasion Johnny met Cassie and me coming home from school. He'd been to the smithy to shoe Jenny, auntie's favourite horse, a creature that would answer to her name and come galloping up to the house. On this day Johnny asked if I wanted to ride Jenny. I said yes, quite delighted because Jenny was the mildest of horses. I got on, no stirrup or bridle, and said, "You won't make it gallop will you?" "No," he replied. "Just take the ears." But he walloped Jenny with his hand, and off she went. I clung on, screaming, holding grimly on to those ears. Johnny laughed and laughed, but I was terrified, and I don't know how I kept on.

'However, auntie saw the incident from the house as Jenny galloped up the rough road, with me holding on like grim death. Johnny, now realising he was in trouble, stopped laughing abruptly and began to run after me, shouting, *"Cydia yn ei fwng!"* (Hold on to its mane). Auntie silenced him with a wave of her hand, and shouted for Jenny to stop. This she did so suddenly that I almost sailed over her head. Somehow, however, I stayed on. There followed a most awful scolding for poor Johnny. He was almost sacked on the spot, but he quickly apologised and all was well.'

The girls' uncle, a witty and amusing man, was a fervent Liberal. He had a picture of Lloyd George on the living room wall, and what the children knew of Lloyd George, of the Liberal Party and of politics in general came from their uncle. He always went around the house in stockinged feet, toes and heels different shades of grey with their constant re-toeing and re-heeling. One evening he had gone to change for chapel. Cassie, who used to help in the house had polished the floor and stairs to a high gloss. The next thing they heard was a bump, in fact a succession of bumps, down the stairs. They rushed out to find him gasping for breath, holding his backside, lying on his back at the foot of the stairs. 'Serves you right,' said his wife, 'for not wearing shoes in the house.'

There were two maids, one elderly, Elin Jones, a weatherbeaten woman, short and stocky, very mannish in her ways, in her voice and appearance and with a loping walk. She wore a man's cap all the time, and she always ate alone in her own small kitchen. 'Uncle never had much to say to her,' says Elsie, 'but auntie liked her, partly because they both came from the same village.'

In the yard outside there was a boiler-house where Elin Jones boiled potatoes in their skins to feed to the pigs and hens. The potatoes were thrown in as they were, into the huge boiler with a great fire underneath. 'Cassie and I used to love to go in with a fork and stab a potato or two on to a plate,' says Elsie. 'Then we would dash into the dairy for a lump of butter, finally running around the back to sit on the grass to enjoy a delicious outdoor meal, tasting even better because it was stolen! More often than not, though, Elin Jones would catch us, and grumble at us for pinching her potatoes. I swear she used to count them and know exactly how many were left in that boiler!

'Of course as children we were always hungry,' continues Elsie. 'We used to go down to the lower field to dig up young turnips and carrots. We would wash them under the outside tap and eat them raw. We also dug for *cnau daear* (wild nuts), with dainty white flowers on top. They were rugged and knobbly and we ate them there and then. They were delicious, as were the blackberries we ate by the pound. We even ate the orange peel that visitors threw away. If mother had known we would have been spanked.'

Cae Du was situated in an idyllic location, high on the hills behind the town, with fields sloping down towards the glorious seascape of Cardigan Bay. Five boys worked there: John Rees, who looked after the horses; Johnny; Jack; one other who seemed to change regularly; and the *gwas bach*, the youngster who did the numerous small jobs considered too 'lowly' by the others. There was Elin Jones, too, whose job it was to feed the pigs and hens and do rough housework. 'Cassie, Beattie and I,' says Elsie, 'used to watch the boys as they strolled to town after their work was done. In the dusk of summer evenings they would wear glow-worms in their caps, for in those days the shimmer of glow-worms on the grass verges was like fairyland, and as the boys moved off down the lane they looked just like clusters of bobbing lights. We girls tried to follow suit by wearing them in our hair, but this was a distinctly unpopular move with auntie who had the task of trying to comb them out.

'Haytime, in particular, was an exciting period. It always seemed to be sunny. Each farm helped other farms by lending carts, horses and men, the carts often being on runners rather than wheels because of the hilly nature of the ground. We loved to go on top of the hay in the barn, for our job was to take the hay as it was pitchforked from the haywain and put it into the loft. At mealtimes cans of tea, usually cold, buttermilk, mounds of bread and butter and cake were brought by the maids to the men in the fields. They would then take their break, and sit with their great hands clasped around their mugs, eating and talking. We loved just being there, teasing and being teased. They were happy times. Other days would be spent on other farms, not

105

Haytime.

Gwynedd Archives Services

helping perhaps as much as we thought or ought, but larking about a great deal.'

No haymaking would ever be carried out on Sundays, of course, although they all enjoyed one well-known tale of a farmer who, behind with his work, decided to risk the wrath of the Almighty by trying to catch up on the Sabbath. But no sooner had he and his three sons got out into the fields than the sun went behind a cloud and there was a loud clap of thunder. 'It's no use, lads,' he shouted, already running for home, 'He's seen us. Follow me!'

Another big event was the October threshing. A threshing machine (*injan ddyrnu*) would be hired to thresh the wheat and a small army of men from neighbouring farms to help, with a great feast to end the day, a hot meal because it was autumn.

'Cae Du's hospitality was renowned,' says Elsie. 'Auntie and the other farmers' wives would have already peeled potatoes and mounds of vegetables the night before, all to be put into a cauldron over a roaring fire. Vast loaves of bread were baked in the big oven in the boiler-house. The following day, after hard work in the fields, weary and tired, yet in great good humour, the men would come into the kitchen to eat. This was a large room, with a stove range, black and always shining. There were two Welsh dressers on opposite walls with meat dishes and plates of all sizes, all in blue. The tables would groan with the weight of food. There was roast beef, roast lamb, goose, pork. There were carrots, sprouts, turnips, roast and mashed potatoes, and there would be rice pudding to follow, plum pudding, bread pudding and apple tarts galore. Sitting down to the meal was a memorable occasion, with much laughter and high spirits, with the youngsters eating last. Jack would then start things going by playing the mouth organ, the men joining in and the singing would go on most of the night.'

Working and feasting went on for two days or more and, when it was all over, the Thanksgiving Service *(Diolchgarwch)* took place, always on the third Monday in October.

'One harvest-time,' says Laura, 'uncle hired an extra hand, a man in his twenties, who was related to Elin Jones. I was about thirteen, and each evening I used to hurry home from school to help. One day he and I got separated from the others who were working in adjoining fields. This youth began to touch me, saying how pretty I was. Then, without warning, he threw me on to a mound of hay and dropped on top of me. I screamed and screamed in terror and suddenly, almost from nowhere, Elin Jones appeared, armed with a pitchfork. *"Cer o'ma'r cythraul,"* she yelled, *"neu mi ladda i di"* (Get out of here you devil, or I'll kill you). She dragged him off, and he needed no more telling with that pitchfork poised so menacingly. She was much stronger than he was and, holding him by the scruff of the neck and taking the responsibility entirely into her own hands, she sacked him on the spot and told him to get away from Cae Du. He flew!'

'Uncle was the shortest man in Harlech,' says Elsie, 'and he was teased by everybody about it. I, too, was small and didn't seem to grow. Mother used to say that I would be like uncle, which upset me and made me cry because I knew the fun that people made of him. But he was bright as a button, and quick witted and charming with it. He had an answer for everything and a joke for all. In chapel he could bring tears to the congregation's eyes while he prayed and when he made the announcements at the end of the service he made them laugh. Auntie used to tell him it was wicked to make people laugh in

107

chapel. She didn't think it was right. But he carried on doing it, and people carried on laughing.

'Uncle was quite mean,' continues Elsie, 'never digging deeply into his pocket. You got a penny on Fair Day but in his mind that had to last for a whole year. As we sat around the kitchen table at tea-time he used to say, "Those who eat more bread and butter and jam get more cake." Thus encouraged, we would eat mounds of bread and butter— only to find that we had left no room at all for cake. Uncle caught us out this way many times and he must have saved himself a great deal of money by doing so! He was no farmer, for auntie was the real farmer. *His* great love was reading; he read deeply and had a great fund of knowledge. Had he had an education he would have made a wonderful Member of Parliament.

'Like many countrymen he could judge the coming weather, and often with amazing accuracy. I remember one cold winter's day the ground was so hard underfoot that it seemed to ring in echo to our footsteps. I met uncle coming out of the barn and he said, *"Mae'r ddaear yn galed, Elsie; mae'r eira wedi gwneud ei wely"* (The ground is hard, Elsie, the snow has made its bed). I've never forgotten that memorable phrase; certainly I can still recall the depth of the winter that followed.

'One day I was sent to look for him because the man from Spiller's had come to see him about cattle feed. Eventually, after much search-ing and shouting, I found him under a tree, hat on head, reading a book of poetry. "Auntie wants you," I said. "Well, all right, but don't you dare tell her where you found me." He gave me a broad smile and the merest hint of a wink!

'He delivered milk each morning to the big houses. Maybe auntie would ask for something else to be done on the way but invariably, with talking to all and sundry, he would forget. On Sundays he went to chapel, of course, and on these days Cassie and I used to take milk to Crown Lodge after our own Sunday School. Auntie would meet us half way and hand us four cans, two of cream and two of milk. It was over a mile to walk and each Sunday we were warned not to be late. "See that you're there by four o'clock." That would be in time for Sunday afternoon tea, and for the six months I lived at Cae Du, rain, hail or snow we got there by tea-time.

Elsie at the door of Crown Lodge, now a students' hostel of Coleg Harlech.

'Except once. One bitter cold day, just before Christmas, we found that we were a little later than usual, having dawdled somewhat in the snow. Scurrying, trying hard not to spill a drop, we went up the drive-way, looking forward to the warmth of the kitchen. Our mouths were watering at the thought of our usual treat—a choice of cake or ginger bread from the large silver tray lying on the scrubbed table. I always chose gingerbread, fresh, with almonds on top. This day, however, our progress was delayed still further in that two of the More children, Miss Peggy and Master George, and a relation, Master Brian, barred our way. They were armed with sticks and branches and they began to hit us, quite severely. We began to cry, not just in pain, but in despair at the thought of being late and missing our gingerbread. To make matters worse we could hear cook shouting for us to hurry up. The next thing we saw was rescue arriving in the shape of the nanny striding down the drive towards us. "Miss Peggy, Master George, I've seen what's been going on. How dare you! Put those sticks away, and just you apologise to Cassie and Elsie for what you've done. There's no tea for you." They did apologise, and we were quite shocked and not a little embarrassed at their having to apologise to us. But we were saved from further embarrassment by being told off ourselves for being late in the first place.

'The next Sunday was the one before Christmas, and we certainly didn't dally that day! On our arrival, to our surprise and delight, not only did we have double helpings of gingerbread, but also Miss Peggy asked us into the hall where we were asked to choose two books each from a selection on the table. I chose *Waifs and Strays*, a sad and lovely little story, and *Grimm's Fairy Tales*. They were both absolute treasures for years to come.

'That Christmas, 1911,' continues Elsie, 'was perhaps the last Christmas in which I believed in Father Christmas, and when stockings were hung. Auntie teased us. "You'll be lucky if you get anything. I think he'll fill your stockings with cinders." This upset us terribly because we thought we'd been good little girls. But we did have a lovely time after all. Mother sent us from Liverpool pretty pinafores—pink for Cassie, pink also for Beattie, white muslin for me with blue dots, all with frills at the bottom. These would be our Sunday pinnies. She also sent us a cup and saucer filled with sweets, tied with ribbon. There were gloves, too, from our cousin Lily. Then there were the usual oranges, apples, nuts and trinkets bulging in the stockings, and it was wonderful to feel and guess the shapes before we looked inside. Auntie gave us a book each, more than usual because of the circumstances, and it helped the *hiraeth* for mother, especially as we'd been expecting cinders! My best gift was from Laura. For some time she had been in service in Tan-yr-Allt, and on a previous Saturday she'd met us in Porthmadog to take us out to tea. Whilst there she took the three of us, Cassie, Beattie and me, to the toy shop by the station, watching us smilingly as we "oohd" and "aahd" over all the lovely things in there. The result on Christmas Day was that I got a beautiful doll's tea-set, one I'd thrilled over in the shop, and quite the loveliest I'd ever seen.'

Memorable events every year were the hiring fairs. There were two, one in the spring and one in the autumn, in May and November. Children were always given a half day holiday from school. The basic purpose of such fairs was to hire farm labour. Young boys would be dressed in their Sunday best in order to attract the farmers' attention, with caps on their heads and raincoats, neatly folded, over their arms. More often than not they were fresh from school. Those the farmers hired would get a contract for six months, occasionally with some payment in advance. The contract could be broken on either side. 'It was often quite pitiful to see a young boy approach a farmer only to see the farmer shake his head,' says Elsie.

The May hirings would be for the busy months of summer—threshing of wheat, herding of sheep, the gathering of hay. But the November hirings were also important, for there was still plenty to do during the winter months—horses had to be fed, the cows milked, pigs looked after. An extra function at Cae Du was rearing turkeys, the first farm in Harlech to have them. They proved difficult birds to rear, for the chicks had to be fed a special diet of mashed hard-boiled eggs mixed with bran. It seemed to work, for Cae Du turkeys grew big and sturdy. At Christmas extra help was hired to pluck them. The best of the down would be kept, dried and cleansed in the ovens, then it would be put into linen flour bags to be sold as pillows.

The loveliest sight at the fairs was always the stallions, brushed and groomed to parade in front of the farmers, like the boys, to attract bids for hiring. People would stand for hours to watch the horses prance by, with brasses gleaming and be-ribboned tails held high.

The fairs came into their own at night, especially perhaps in the autumn. Now, in the rapidly advancing gloom, the stall-keepers would light their paraffin lamps which would then swing to and fro in

111

the wind, throwing a warm and comforting glow all around. As the evening wore on and the day's work ended the farmhands came down from the hilltop farms. 'Many, short of money as they were, would give us pennies,' says Laura. 'This, when added to what we'd managed to save for the fair through the year, gave us quite a bit to spend.'

There were perhaps two or three dozen stalls in all. There would be one selling cheap jewellery, others selling crockery and clothing, certainly a number selling 'India Rock' as it was called. There was pure mint rock, others of different flavours, but the best was the famous dark brown 'Llannerch-y-medd Rock' from Anglesey, a recipe held secret for generations in one family. It was sold by an old lady in a pure white bonnet, who would cut it into small pieces for people to try, shouting: *"Rŵan am damed o roc o Lannerch-y-medd"* (Now for a piece of rock from Llannerch-y-medd). The children would come back again and again, often ending up with a bagful! Always, too, there was a coconut stall. 'Auntie loved coconuts,' says Laura, 'and Jack was the most accurate thrower in the town. She would personally take him to the fair and pay him to get her some coconuts. Indeed, other people would do the same. "That one, Jack, now that one," Auntie would say. "Look lady," the proprietor would say eventually, as Jack kept knocking the coconuts off their pedestals, "I'll give you money to take the lad away. He's taking all my profit".'

One of the most colourful events of the fair was held towards the end, and that was the Indian fire swallower. He attracted great crowds, and cries of wonderment would rise up as the flames seemed to disappear down his throat. He was always vigorously clapped at the end, and coins would be thrown on to his cloak by an appreciative audience. After this the fair would gradually wind down. 'We children, however, always left until the very last moment the best thing of all, and that was—chips,' says Beattie. 'The chip van used to send out lovely mouth-watering smells all evening, and excitedly we'd queue up for a large bagful, costing a ha'penny, of the best chips ever.' Both Laura and Elsie agree! They and their friends would sit on a low wall, taking warmth from the bags themselves, tucking into those chips with gusto, while the breath from a dozen hungry mouths climbed the cold night air in clouds.

Then, one by one, those swinging lamps were dowsed.

CHAPTER 11

Cwm Bychan

As described by Laura:

'In the hills above the town there is a small valley *(cwm bychan)*. In this valley lies a lake, clear and tranquil, reflecting in its calm waters the gentle outlines of the hills above. There are woods of birch, larch and oak, expanses of heath and fern. There are rocky knolls, open glades, coombes and hollows. No wonder it has been described as an 'Upland Arcady'. It was, and still is, a favourite spot for picnics, for large parties, organised and noisy with children's games, or for small groups, or for lovers wanting to get away from the town far below. There are trout and salmon in the fresh streams running through the valley, which, caught and cooked on fires of gorse and dried fern, as we did, sent out the most wonderful aromas. Even today, nearly seventy years on, I can still smell that marvellous mixture of burning bracken and twigs. It seemed to stay in the senses for days. It was heavenly, too, to breathe in that fresh mountain air which made us so ravenously hungry. On would go more twigs to hurry things on!

'A particular memory of this enchanting spot was of a picnic my friend Merdeg and I shared there with our cousin Owen, a seafarer from Liverpool. He had travelled the world, to Rio, Martinique, Guadeloupe and the South Seas, but he said the harmony of mountain and sky at Cwm Bychan, the purity of the air and the tranquil calmness of the lake were unmatched anywhere in the world. That day the birds sang, the bees hummed and dragonflies darted above the fast flowing streams. None of us spoke until the whistle of the kettle told us it was time for tea. We sat there, eating and talking, and soon Owen, a talented artist, took out his sketch-pad and with lovely swift pencil strokes drew Merdeg as she lay there, with a book in her hand. It was a beautiful drawing, and to see it now would bring back such a flood of lovely memories. The summer day was long and lazy as we strayed along the narrow paths, past waterfalls and with the sweet scent of flowers in our nostrils, until the gathering shadows told us that it was time to pack our picnic basket and start for home. Now it was all downhill, and I will never forget coming over those gentle hills

Plas Amherst servants' picnic.

Dudley Maidment collection

as the sun went down slowly over the bay, with Merdeg and me
singing, "When the golden sun sinks in the West". As we sang we
gathered saucer-like mushrooms which we were to enjoy later in a
glorious supper fit to end the most memorable of days.

'One sad event connected with this lovely lake concerned an elderly
and charming bachelor, a Mr. Davies, the Mr. Davies who made
ginger beer. He seemed drawn to the lake, for every Sunday he would
walk, whatever the weather, to and from its shores. On fine days he
would sit on the slopes overlooking the lake for hours on end, reading
and dreaming. Sadly, the lake must have drawn him closer and closer
for he later committed suicide in those still waters.

'Despite this sadness, however, the memories of Cwm Bychan lake
are treasured ones, as they must still be for those who visit its shores
today.

'In later years I composed an Ode to Cwm Bychan:

115

O, secret brook, 'midst banks of green,
You call as in some waking dream.
From high hill top to lowland dell
What age-old stories do you tell?

With hidden laughter in your song,
Soft music as you roll along,
Your voice it seems at one with mine
Intoxicates like sparkling wine.

Full seventy years I've shared with you
Sweet times of joy and sorrow too.
My secret thoughts I know you'll keep
Through all the years of death's long sleep.

Till then I long for wings to fly
And join the lark that sings on high,
To add to his my own bright song
Above this place where I belong.

Warm suns have passed, and winters deep,
Yet you, dear hills, proud vigil keep,
And scenes as nature's child I knew
Reach out to fill my heart anew.'

CHAPTER 12

Wartime

The Great War started on August Bank Holiday Monday 1914. Harlech was full of visitors and in one boarding house, Dros-y-Môr, a regular army officer by the name of Reid was on holiday with his wife, three children and nanny. On the Bank Holiday Sunday a telegram for Major Reid arrived at the Post Office. News of this soon travelled around Harlech and the telegraph boy was followed, as always, by a crowd of children, keenly inquisitive about news so exciting that it couldn't wait for the normal post. Knowing the importance of his position, the telegraph boy swaggered up to the front door of Dros-y-Môr and rang the bell. The door was opened by the nanny, who accepted the telegram. By the afternoon the news had swept around the town that Major Reid had been recalled to his Regiment and would be leaving shortly. Spectators gathered and waited. Soon a pony and trap arrived. Major Reid came out, now transformed in khaki, got into the trap and, waving goodbye to a tearful wife and children, was driven away to catch the five o'clock train. It was a short burst of excitement for the children of Harlech, made a little sad with the departure of his family a few days later, and saddened still further some weeks afterwards when news came through that he had been killed in France.

Before the war numerous foreigners came regularly to Harlech and, as the war went on, people began to wonder if they had been spies. It was hardly likely but, with the passage of time, such suspicions grew stronger.

One man, a large cheerful Hungarian, brought with him a big, black bear, muzzled and chained. To the strains of a hurdy-gurdy the bear would dance, or shuffle, holding a tin mug into which spectators would put small coins. Say 'Thank you,' his master would command, and the bear then emited a great groaning sound. The children loved it, although it probably scared them stiff.

'There were barrel organists, and we'd dance around them in time to their lovely melodies,' says Laura. 'They always brought a monkey and he was full of tricks. He danced and pranced and jumped on our

117

shoulders, to our screams of delight. Often people would shout, "Where's Laura? Come on, Laura. Do the Can-Can!" And I would respond, having picked up the steps in Liverpool. Being just about the only one in Harlech able to do it, I would dance from one end of the street to the other, my skirts held high to all the clapping and cheering and with my hair flying all over the place.'

Gipsies brought love birds who told fortunes for a penny. Older girls, giggling or demure, would give the gipsy a coin and the birds picked out cards with their 'fortunes' on and presented them to the blushing girls. 'We thought it was great,' says Elsie. 'Those gipsies brought lots of joy to our Welsh towns and villages.' But were they and the other strangers spies?

Each summer in the years before the war there was a Boys' Brigade camp on Morfa Harlech. These boys came from Manchester or, more exactly, Salford, and they were called the 'Salford Lads' by the locals. At Church Parade on Sundays, smart in their dark blue, they attracted a lot of attention, from the girls especially. 'I remember Laura meeting two or three of the lads one summer,' says Elsie. 'She'd been given a lovely hat by Lady Gladys—pink straw with multicoloured flowers and with a ribbon of deeper pink at the back. She wore it so proudly while walking on the beach with the boys, looking the very picture of a Gainsborough Lady. However, she apparently never told them that she was in service, preferring to lay claim to being from one of the big houses on the hill. One evening, however, I was playing outside our cottage when the boys came strolling by. Looking through our open door, they spied that hat on a hallway peg. "Eeh, bah goom," shouted one, "there's Laura's 'at!" I forget the outcome, but I think it was the end of the affair!

'I recall a similar occasion,' continues Elsie, 'when Beattie and her friend Nora, both young schoolgirls, were required to bring two sacks of potatoes and carrots on the train—a gift from Nora's farmer uncle to her mother in Harlech. They were quite heavy and the two girls struggled to heave them on board. While on the train they, too, met some of the lads and when they arrived in Harlech, still flirting outrageously, they disowned the two bags and airily left them on the train! Again I forget the outcome, but I'm sure it must have been amusing—to those watching!'

Of course, there was some resentment, perhaps natural, from the local boys over the development of these summer relationships. Gradually, however, over the years, jealousy gave way to friendship and by the summers of 1913 and 1914 there were campfire sing-songs, with the Salford Lads and the Welsh boys singing their songs each in turn.

In an astonishing coincidence during a lull in the fighting at Gallipoli in 1915, some of the Harlech boys in the 1st/7th Royal Welch Fusiliers were singing around a camp fire on that distant shore when, around a bluff, came a group of soldiers wearing the 'Fleur-de-lys' of the Manchester Regiment. They came up to the Welshmen and said, 'You're not by chance from Harlech, are you?' and before the conversation got any further they recognised each other as former rivals, then friends, from a time that seemed long ago. And so, on a still Turkish night, the boys from Harlech and the lads from Salford sat around their camp fires on that far-off peninsula and, once again, sang the same songs that had charmed the air in the tranquil peace of those half-forgotten summers.

In the early months of the War thousands of refugees from Belgium were scattered all over Britain. 'A large number came to Harlech,' says Elsie, 'and auntie had a big family of them, some eight or nine, in Clogwyn Villa.' Others stayed in the Graves' house, Erinfa, Perceval Graves being away in London at the time and Robert Graves a subaltern in the Royal Welch Fusiliers. Robert Owen, W. H. More's Secretary, was the Secretary of the Refugees' Committee. He regularly took them for walks and then brought them back home for tea. One of the refugees, Count Max de Maude, painted a water colour of old Antwerp and presented it to Mr. Owen. It still hangs in his daughter Bessie's house now. People in the bigger houses gave parties and here again there were exchanges of song, when Welsh folk melodies intermingled with Belgian peasant music. 'They were lovely people, though sad,' says Elsie.

One day there was great excitement in the town when two German prisoners-of-war were caught. They had escaped from a camp in mid-Wales and a local farmer saw them sitting by the river in Llanbedr, three miles away. He spoke to them but when they did not reply, either in Welsh or English, he became suspicious. He pedalled away

119

on his bicycle and contacted the police. Eventually they were captured and brought to Harlech. The news, as always, spread quickly and crowds gathered, adults as well as children, with anticipation mounting by the minute. In due course the prisoners arrived and just as quickly the excitement evaporated. 'What we'd been expecting, I don't know,' says Elsie, 'but we certainly hadn't expected them to look so ordinary. They were just like us. It was a real letdown. However, they were treated with great kindness by the police. Although they were handcuffed there was no forced marching to impress onlookers.'

A rather gruesome event was the washing ashore in October and November 1917 of three bodies from the sea. For some days they lay wrapped in tarpaulin on tables in the church hall. At first they were thought to be German submariners. Later, however, they were identified as British sailors from an unknown ship sunk in the Irish Sea. They were buried reverently in the churchyard. One other body was washed ashore a year later, in September 1918.

'At the beginning of the war Jack was home from sea, and had been for some weeks,' says Elsie. 'In the hiring fair of November (1914) there was a Recruiting Sergeant doing a different kind of hiring, with the famous Kitchener poster behind him. His was one of the most popular stalls, and many of the boys of the town joined the Colours that day and got the King's shilling. At home mother was making tea and the kettle was singing merrily on the hob. Jack walked in, smiling, and quietly placed the shilling on the table. Immediately tears came into mother's eyes. "You've joined?" "Yes," was his proud response. He named all those who had joined with him, nearly all of whom were to be posted to the 1st/7th Battalion, Royal Welch Fusiliers, and who were destined for the Dardanelles.'

From then on things seemed to move very fast indeed. Jack and all his comrades went away for training, and then they were home again for Christmas, seven glorious days. The day then dawned for their departure, all now in khaki, some still self-conscious. They formed up in the town at about four o'clock in the dark of a late-December afternoon, with what remained of the town band, young boys and old men, in front. The band struck up and they moved off, the men marching smartly down the steep slope to the station to catch the five o'clock

Jack (left) in pre-war days.

Author's collection

Harlech station: the start point of journeys both sad and gay.

Author's collection

121

train. The whole town seemed to be there to see them off. There was shouting and cheering and the waving of flags. It seemed as if they were going on a day trip, just like the old days. 'But already mother was in tears and soon, after the train had gone, a strange desolation came over us all, and many others were now openly weeping,' says Elsie. 'We couldn't believe they'd gone, that Jack had gone to war. In many ways he was the mainstay of the family. Although he was only twenty-one he was almost like a father, being so much older than we were.'

As the weeks rolled on news from the various war fronts came in, the major source of such news in Harlech being the *Liverpool Echo*, like all other newspapers with its pages and pages of casualty lists. The only time when many children were allowed out on winter evenings was to fetch the *Echo* when it arrived from Liverpool on the seven o'clock train. 'Crowds of us went down to the station to fetch copies of the paper,' says Elsie, 'and despite the sadness of the news there was still fun on the way home. In the blackness of those winter evenings the boys would be waiting and hiding, jumping out at the girls from different places. We were scared stiff, all the way up the hill and home.'

The first months of the war passed. 'By now I was eighteen years old,' says Laura, 'and very much in love with Griff Roberts (or Griff "Pencerrig" as he was more usually known, after the name of his house). He was so handsome with such a lovely sense of humour. A fine musician, he played the piano, violin, organ and cornet, and for many years both before and after the war he was the conductor of the then-famed Harlech Silver Band, the same band that had marched the boys off to war. We would walk together on the beach, laughing and joking, holding each other close, strolling barefoot along the shore. I don't think there could ever have been anyone happier than we were, for the flowers bloomed and the birds sang only for us. He volunteered soon after the outbreak of war and went with the Royal Welch Fusiliers to the Near East and Salonika, and although he was one of those who came home four years later and thus was not part of the awful statistics of over one million dead, nevertheless our relationship was a tragedy of those years, for it never again reached the heights of the lovely summers of 1913 and 1914.'

122

And so Harlech, as every other town and village in England, Scotland, Ireland and Wales, agonised through those long months and years as they passed slowly and painfully. But even that most awful of wars in due course came to an end and the boys returned home, although 420 officers and over 10,000 men of the Royal Welch Fusiliers did not, twenty-one of the young men of Harlech amongst them, having been killed on the shores of Gallipoli, in Salonika, in Mesopotamia, in the fields of France and Belgium and on the high seas. There were Peace celebrations in the castle and, as the senior Royal Welch Fusilier of Harlech, Captain Robert Graves spoke about the glorious dead, commending the Welsh as fighting men and receiving loud cheers.

Of those that did return some were embittered, others just glad to be home, but all trying to pick up the threads of their previous life. But there is little doubt that those four dreadful years were a watershed in every way. Life would never be the same as it had been in those halcyon days before the war.

EPILOGUE

Men of Harlech

The Harlech War Memorial reads as follows:

In Memory of
The Men of Harlech
who fell in the Great War
1914-1918

Gwilym Bevers—Tremorthin

Douglas Davies—Caereinion

Evan Evans—Brwynllynnau

William J. Hughes—Tan Rallt

David W. Humphreys—Station House

Thomas Jones—Llechwedd Canol

Edward Jones—Hendre

Evan Lloyd—Tynymaes

Ellis Owen—Moriah Terrace

R.Lewis Owen—Moriah Terrace

George Owen—Fforddgroes

William Owen—Fforddgroes

Matthew Owen—Waterloo House

William Owen—Llechwedd Canol

Owen Parry—Grogan Terrace

Leon Rees Roberts—Bronwen Terrace

Morris Thomas—Grogan Terrace

J. Griffith Williams—Bronwen Terrace

Richard Williams—Rosslyn House

Robert J. Williams— Tynybarth

Griffith Jones—Llechwedd Canol

★   ★   ★

Twenty-one young men of Harlech died in the First World War. A short account of the life, and death, of four of them is recounted over the next few pages, with the story of five who came back. Happily, two are still alive and, almost as a bridge, link our end-of-century consciousness to those Edwardian summers when they themselves were in the first flush of youth.

124

JACKIE WILLIAMS

Born in 1893, Jackie was three years older than Laura, ten years older than Elsie and thirteen years older than Beattie. To them he was the ideal elder brother, always helpful, generous and kind. All three sisters looked forward to Sunday evenings when he came home from the farm. Before supper he would amuse them, play games with them and make them laugh. Then they would watch him as he sat down to supper, a piece of rabbit pie, perhaps, that had been saved from lunchtime, followed by fruit tart or rice pudding.

Although Jackie was away at sea from the age of seventeen it was still a shock when he decided to join the army in 1914, at the age of twenty-one. The night before he left a small group of young men gathered outside the house, some of them due to leave with him the following day. They shuffled uncomfortably, embarrassed at first, then they began to sing. Their young voices swelled in the night as they sang familiar songs, both sad and gay. 'Mother held back her tears until they began to sing "Goodnight Sweetheart",' says Elsie. 'Then she broke down. The gap Jack was to leave in our household was felt by all of us. It was like a light going out.'

He joined the 1st/7th Battalion, Royal Welch Fusiliers, a battalion in which there was a large number of local men from Harlech and the surrounding areas. The next few months passed quickly and he was promoted to Corporal. He returned on leave two or three times, and when he was home it was almost like it used to be, with laughter and games and tears at his leaving. He then wrote to say that they had received orders to prepare for service overseas, and that most suspected they were going to the Dardanelles, to try 'something different' in order to bring that stagnant campaign to a successful conclusion.

By August 1915 the battalion had landed on the shores of Gallipoli, at Suvla Bay, and there, alongside the 5th and 6th Battalions, the 1st/7th fought in those grim and terrible battles until, after continual heartbreaking failure, the whole Expeditionary Force was eventually withdrawn early in 1916.

By 1917 all three battalions were fighting in Gaza and were involved in the three Gaza battles in the spring and autumn of that year. Conditions there were bleak, for not only did they have to contend with the enemy's fierce resistance, but also with the stultifying heat. For most of the time the Jehamsin blew, the hot wind from the deserts of the interior, bringing with it a fine mist of stinging sand. Men were laid low with fever and thirst, for they were only allowed one bottle of water per day.

It was in Gaza, during the first battle, on 26th/27th March, that Jackie was badly wounded. In great pain he lay on the battlefield until, eventually, he slipped into unconsciousness. Many hours later, after much patient searching, he was found by two friends, Ianto Humphreys, later also to be badly wounded, and John Williams, from Llanbedr, who was to be killed in that same battle. Ianto and John found Jackie lying in a pool of blood. They picked him up, even though they thought he was dead, and despite heavy Turkish machine-gun fire they managed to carry him back to the British lines, to a dressing station which had been set up under the walls of a mosque. There they found some lingering signs of life, and eventually he was transported on a long and painful journey overland, first by camel and then by lorry, to the British Military Hospital in Alexandria. A vein in his neck had been severed by shrapnel. His shoulder, too, was shattered, and really there didn't seem much hope for him. Death seemed to be only a matter of time and he was in constant delirium. However, surgeons did what they could and performed at first what was meant to be a temporary operation, tying silver wire around the vein.

Jackie was in Alexandria for many months. Medical cards were sent home at regular intervals, each with the bare phrase: 'On the Danger List'. The visits of Sam Postman were dreaded more and more. Sam, having read the card, would come along whistling, trying to soften the blow before passing it over. 'Jackie still not too good, Mrs. Williams.' One day, however, his familiar whistle was replaced by a whoop of joy. 'Good news, Mrs Williams,' he shouted. 'Jackie is off the danger list.' She wept and wept for joy. Her spirits rose and kept on rising as cards now came regularly to state that he was 'improving' all the time.

In due course a letter arrived to say that he had been brought home to England and was in Fazakerley Hospital, Liverpool. 'No sooner had the news reached us,' says Elsie, 'than mother had packed a case and was on the way to Liverpool to see him. She stayed there with her sister, with Beattie and me being left with Mrs. Owen, Waterloo House, for a few days.'

'I was in Liverpool at the time,' says Laura, 'and I rushed to the hospital when I heard the news. He was cheerful but looked ghastly. He was dreadfully wounded but the operation those wonderful surgeons had performed in Alexandria had been very successful. Even the doctors and nurses at Fazakerley Hospital told me that he had been dubbed "the miracle man", and it was decided that the "temporary" surgery of wrapping silver wire around the vein should remain. Indeed, it remained there for the rest of his life.'

Jack after the war.

'Then,' says Elsie, 'it was Beattie's turn and mine to go to Liverpool, but instead of visiting him in hospital, Jack came to see us, dressed in his blue hospital uniform and red tie. He looked awful, like death, and he was still in great pain. For years to come the shoulder wound would open and puss seep out. Eventually he lost much of the use of his left arm.'

On his return to Harlech in the summer of 1918 he was welcomed with great enthusiasm and affection by the townspeople, for he was popular and well-liked. He obtained light work as a postman and from his visits to the upland farms he always came back laden with butter and eggs. In 1920 he married Ida, a cousin from Liverpool, herself a young war widow with two children, eventually having four children of his own, all girls. In later years he became gatekeeper at the castle, and then opened a fish and chip shop which became well-known locally. 'Jackie's chips' are recalled with pleasure to this day.

In 1953 he caught a cold which rapidly turned to pneumonia. He died that Easter at the age of sixty, still known as 'the miracle man' because of the way he had fought back from almost certain death thirty-six years before.

IANTO HUMPHREYS

Ianto Humphreys was born in 1895 and in the years before the First World War he went to South Wales to find work in the coal mines. There he worked in the Ystrad Gelli pit, although his family continued to live in Harlech, and it was to Harlech that Ianto came on his holidays. It was while on holiday that he enlisted in 1914, at Crown Lodge, where Mary Pugh whom he was eventually to marry worked as a maid. Along with many other local boys he joined the 1st/7th Royal Welch Fusiliers, seeing action in the late summer of 1915 in the Dardanelles Campaign.

The heat there was unbearable, with trenches like ovens and grass so withered that the hot wind kicked up a constant dust. All around was confusion as orders contradicted orders. There was constant tension and a sense of ever-present shock, understandable when young boys were transported from one environment to another so

Ianto Humphreys before the war.

Ianto (left) in Palestine, 14th August 1917 (with Lance Corporal's stripe apparently sewn upside down!)

Gwilym Humphreys' collection

130

violently different. It was no wonder that, of the 50,000 men who landed at Suvla, 18,000 were casualties, mainly medical, in the first three days. In all 22,000 sick and wounded had to be evacuated. Hospitals in Malta and Egypt were filled to overflowing, and the *Aquitania*, the famous ship on which the children had 'sailed' in those childhood games so long ago, and other vessels like her had to ferry thousands of the wounded directly back to England.

It was later on, after the withdrawal from Gallipoli and in the First Battle of Gaza, that Ianto, along with John Williams, saved the life of Jackie Williams who had been left for dead on the battlefield. Always the most caring of men, Ianto was looked up to by his companions because he was like a father to those around him. Although not much older than they were he was at all times a calming influence in the most trying of circumstances.

His companion, John Williams, was killed a short time later during the Third Battle of Gaza and lies buried at Beersheba. In those twelve days of fierce and almost continuous hand-to-hand fighting the British and Turkish trenches were at times only twenty-five yards apart. It was in this battle that Ianto himself was badly wounded, with a bullet piercing one lung and grazing the other. He was taken to hospital in Alexandria where he lay seriously ill for many months, being brought home by hospital ship in the autumn of 1918.

In later years Ianto would tell how he remembered spinning around with the impact of that bullet. He thought he was dying, and it wasn't far from the truth because the bullet passed only an inch or so from his heart and out at the back, tearing a great hole on its way. Occasionally, when asked by friends, he would show them that gaping hole.

In 1921 he married Mary Pugh, whom he had courted gently for nearly three years. Afterwards he worked as a labourer in the castle and during the repairs to the St. David's Hotel after the fire there of 1922. He tried working as a miner again in South Wales, but his deteriorating health was against him. He returned to Harlech and played a remarkably full part in the social life of the town. Despite his condition, he played trombone in the Harlech Silver Band and was a Founder-Member of the Harlech Labour Party. Indeed, the Labour Party flourished in Harlech in the years after the First World War and rapidly replaced the Liberals as the favoured Party. This was due in

Mary Pugh, 1985.

no small way to the socialist leanings of returning soldiers, especially those who had fought in the Near East and who were exceptionally bitter about the inept handling of the Dardanelles Campaign, the lack of leadership there and consequent loss of life.

Ianto's health declined still further, and he began to spend an increasing amount of time in the sanatoria of Talgarth and Denbigh. Tuberculosis set in and he died in 1927, aged thirty-two, leaving Mary with three children, Robert, Gwilym and Maldwyn. Mary had a dreadfully hard life thereafter, taking in mending and washing where she could. Unfortunately the Army pension that Ianto had been receiving died with him for pensions could not be paid to widows of those ex-servicemen who had married after the war. But she remembered the kindness of Harlech people who, although poor themselves, helped in any way they could.

A few months after Ianto's death Mary began to receive mysterious envelopes at regular intervals, each containing a ten-shilling note. That money was a god-send and helped in so many ways during her long widowhood. It was many years later that she found that those anonymous gifts had come from Jackie Williams, whose life Ianto had saved all those years before in the bitter Gaza battles.

MATTHEW OWEN

Matthew Owen was born in 1887, the eldest of a family of eight children consisting of two boys and six girls. He is survived by two sisters, Annie, who is hale and hearty at ninety-six and who still lives in Harlech, and Maria, who lives in Stoke Poges.* His younger brother Edward (Ned) died in 1984.

As a young man, Matthew was thoughtful, popular and generous. (Annie remembers him sending £7 home to enable his father to go to Liverpool to see a heart specialist, 'Though father, sadly, died two days later.') Over six feet tall, Matthew was handsome and possessed an impressive physique. In the years before the First World War he worked under W. J. Leaver, at that time the Professional at the Royal

*Now sadly, both dead.

133

St. David's Golf Club, then he left Harlech for Tyldesley Golf Club, near Manchester. Shortly before the outbreak of war he went to North Shields where he became Pro at the golf club there. Those years of caddying and steady apprenticeship seemed now about to come to fruition, and there is no doubt that he would have had a splendid career in the game.

However, soon after war broke out he wrote home and enthusiastically told his mother of his intention to volunteer, enlisting in the Grenadier Guards on 30th November 1914. He transferred to the Welsh Guards amongst hundreds of other Welshmen when that Regiment was formed on 27th February 1915, being given Regimental Number 502. As the only Harlech man to join the Welsh Guards on its formation he must have been proud that 'The March of the Men of Harlech' was selected as the Regimental Slow March.

In due course he came home to Waterloo House, the family home, to say goodbye, but on his return to North Shields and shortly before he went overseas he somewhat unexpectedly got married, on 14th August, at Christ Church, Westminster. He told his mother that he did not really want to get married, but his fiancée had persuaded him, saying that as a wife she would have a better chance of seeing him if he were wounded.

Shortly before the Regiment left for France they were paraded for an inspection visit from His Majesty the King, who expressed his conviction that it would not be long before they won great victories to emblazon on their Colours. They embarked for France on 17th August, three days after Matthew's wedding. His progress in the regiment was rapid and he was promoted Lance Sergeant on 30th August.

Another member of this fine regiment was Captain Osmond Williams ('Ossie') of Deudraeth Castle, near Penrhyn, who had visited the Harlech home of the Earl and Countess of Winchilsea in the years before the First World War and who was now married to their daughter, Lady Gladys.

It had been generally understood that the Welsh Guards would be given the first possible opportunity of winning their spurs. Unlike many other regiments who began their service in France with guard duties and further training, their standard of preparedness and training were considered so good that they went straight into the front line.

It was on Saturday 25th September 1915 that the great battle of Loos began. The first objective that the Welsh Guards were given was to take the hill to the west of Loos. On Monday 27th, in a night operation and in pouring rain the Welshmen attacked a network of German trenches and bomb-proof shelters, and the much-vaunted Prussian Guards were driven back. From there they moved down through the town under severe sniper fire, but their greatest test was still to come with the assault on Hill 70 to the east of Loos, with the Germans in an exceptionally strong and well-nigh impregnable defensive position. Progress now was slower, and the enemy made merciless use of well-hidden machine guns. But the final charge of the Welsh Guards was vigorously and enthusiastically executed, and as they reached the enemy's entrenchments they shouted *'Cymru am byth'* (Wales for ever) and took the hill by bayonet. Thus the Welsh Guards won their first Battle Honour in their first battle.

But all this had not been accomplished without loss. A tragic death was that of Captain Osmond Williams who had been the first to get into the enemy trenches. A much-loved officer, he had led his men with exemplary bravery. In going to the aid of a wounded soldier he had been shot in the shoulder but, thinking the injury minimal, he continued to advance until a second bullet mortally wounded him. He was taken to hospital and was visited there by General Sir John French himself. Captain Osmond Williams died three days later, his death casting great gloom over the whole regiment. Four generals and all the officers of the regiment attended his funeral.

Considering the great deeds of the Welsh Guards that day the number of casualties was relatively small, 171 in all, but amongst them was Matthew Owen, killed leading his section up the final slope of Hill 70.

It was the news of Captain Williams' death that reached Harlech first. Matthew's sister Annie and his mother heard of it at different times, but neither dared mention his death for fear of worrying the other about Matthew's safety. The following day, however, the sad news of Matthew's own death came through. Pat, his widow, travelled overnight from North Shields to be with them but, after waving goodbye to her on the train the following day, they never saw her again. Sadly, Matthew's body was never found, although his name is commemorated on Panel 10 of the Loos Memorial erected shortly after the end of the war between the towns of Lens and Bethune. 'For a long time,' says Annie, 'mother would sit in front of her fire in the early hours of the morning, crying bitterly, but doing so alone so that she could hide her grief from us children.'

'The sorrow of Matthew's death hit our family too,' says Elsie. 'We remembered pre-war days, Mrs. Owen being mother's best friend in Harlech, and memories came flooding back of happy hours spent in the Owen household—of treacle sandwiches, of overnight stays and of Mrs. Owen's charming waywardness with the English language.'

Mrs. Owen died in 1928, never having fully recovered from the tragic loss of her beloved eldest child.

W. O. EVANS

William Evans was born in April 1899. 'When people ask me when I was born,' he says, 'I reply, "Not this century!" '

He left school at fourteen, and although his father was a farmer it was too small a holding to offer employment to William. So he went to the hiring fair at Harlech in May 1913 where he was hired for Tyddyn Du farm, Llanbedr. He was given a shilling by the farmer which he immediately gave to his mother in part payment for the clothes and shoes she had bought him to improve his chances of being taken on.

His wages were £5 for six months, working seven days a week. Sunday work was milking the cows and feeding the horses, with one other boy to help him. This was always followed by evening chapel. The food was good, cooked by the housekeeper. There was bread and milk for breakfast, with tea and bread as a filler. The midday meal would consist of roast lamb or pork, with potatoes and vegetables, followed by rice pudding. The two old bachelor brothers who owned the farm ate at a table in the centre of the large kitchen with the boys at a separate table by the window. Supper at 7 o'clock consisted of a huge bowl of porridge, accompanied by a large jug of buttermilk. At 9 o'clock they went to bed in the stable loft, one big bed in which the two boys slept.

William didn't get his wages until the very last day of the half-year, when David Lloyd Jones, the elder of the two bachelors, gave him five gold sovereigns. He stayed for another six-month period for the same pay, and then he left.

The next May hiring (now 1914) took him to Tyddyn Goronwy, Tal-y-bont, for £8.10s.0d. for six months, then for another six months. Here, an important daily task was to take milk down to the station before breakfast in order to catch the early train to Barmouth. In May 1915 he was hired once more, but he wasn't taken on at the November fair. So, with the war now being over twelve months old, though under age, he decided to join the army, walking the three miles to Crown Lodge to sign on and then walking home again.

Later that month he was sent to Blaenau Ffestiniog and although it was only twelve miles away it was a new experience for him, for he had hardly been away from home before. He was to join 3rd/7th Royal Welch Fusiliers, with headquarters in the old British School. Despite having an aunt in Blaenau he wasn't allowed to stay with her but, along with two others, was billeted with an elderly widow. After three months' training, mostly on the railway station, or so it seemed to him, they were sent to Oswestry, to a large camp with up to 50,000 men in training, a very different world indeed. Here was a man the like of whom William had never met before, Sergeant-Major Aldridge, an old soldier from Bala, called 'Mad Jack'. Big and powerful, he had a foghorn voice that in every way matched his physique.

The army, showing practical concern, gave William a month's leave in the summer of 1916, partly on the death of his mother and partly to help with the hay on the family's smallholding. Indeed, such leave was not infrequent, especially in the first years of the war; it was almost a carry-over from the traditions of eighteenth century warfare. When he went back to camp, William was wearing black braid on one button. Aldridge peered at it.

'What's that for?' he asked.

'My mother's dead,' replied William.

'So's mine,' said Mad Jack. 'Take it off.'

For all his apparent fierceness, Sergeant-Major Aldridge was well-

William Evans (extreme right), Namur, January 1919.

W. O. Evans' collection

'Roses' from the Machine Gun Corps at the end of the war—William Evans, sixth from right, back row.

liked and respected. Besides which, at the end of each day he drilled the young officers, and the soldiers liked that.

William had only been sixteen years old when he joined up. In the autumn of 1916, still too young to go to France, he was transferred from the Royal Welch Fusiliers to the 7th Battalion Manchester Regiment, training in Colchester and Scarborough. In March 1917 he did finally go to France, although he need not have gone for he was still not eighteen. In his first months in France he was not involved in any major action although there were a number of times when he went over the top in trench raids. In July, however, at la Bassine, he received a heavy dose of gas. He went to the base hospital at Etaples where, for a few days, he was sick eight or nine times a day. From there he was sent to England and was in hospital until January 1918, convalescing in Scarborough.

He returned to France in the spring and was transferred to the Machine Gun Corps where he was 'constantly busy' in the final advance as the Number Two on the powerful Vickers machine gun, following the infantry in close support. He recalls vividly the awesome sight of hundreds of dead German bodies lying in their path as they advanced.

William finally came home in April 1919. He farmed for a year, then worked with the Water Board, digging drains. From there he went to Blaenau Ffestiniog, staying this time with his aunt, working in then the world's biggest slate quarry, the Oakley, with a workforce of up to 2,000 men. In the quarry they were divided into teams of four, two rockmen working on the rock and two quarrymen on the machines which split and dressed the slates. Each slate was stamped with the mark of the man who worked it and every month there was intensive bargaining with the steward for the next month's work—perhaps £1 to £2 per week basic pay with an agreed bonus at the end. The bigger the block of slate blown the easier it was to work. William once blew a block big enough for two men to work on for six months.

On one occasion he dropped a lighted candle ('snuffin') on some grains of explosive powder which he had spilled. The resulting explosion luckily (or unluckily for William) 'caused damage to no-one else but me'. Ill, mostly from shock, he was in hospital for a month. He remembers his father coming to see him and standing by the foot of the bed. *'Sut buost ti mor flêr?'* he asked (How could you be so untidy?) *'Mewn pob damwain mae blerwch.'* (In every misfortune there is carelessness.) William could only agree.

He stayed at the Oakley until 1925 when many were sacked because of the reduction in demand for Welsh slate. After some years in London in a variety of jobs and marrying a Welsh nurse there he returned home in 1940 where he farmed until his retirement in 1964. William's latter years were spent in the Old People's Home at Barmouth, some ten miles from Harlech, where, deservedly, he was well cared for. He died in 1988.

DAVID WILLIAM HUMPHREYS

David was one of a family of five brothers and three sisters. Two sisters, Jenny and Gwen, and one brother, Stanley, still live in Harlech. Two brothers, David and Griffith, fought in the First World War. Their father, who worked on the Cambrian Railway, was posted from Shrewsbury to Harlech as Stationmaster in 1913. Jenny remembers at the age of eight standing on the platform on their arrival, looking at the trees around her and at the castle dominating the town; she had only just arrived and already she had no wish to leave. David did not come with the other members of the family for he had joined the Royal Navy the year before, 1912, on a fifteen-year engagement. He had left school at fourteen and worked for the Cambrian Railway in the lamp room, but he hadn't been content, especially as the Navy had attracted him for some time.

David's going to sea broke his mother's heart and she missed him terribly. But she was still proud of him when he returned home on leave. David was very particular about his shoes; they had to be without toecaps and when he was home his mother took him to Barmouth to buy them, with David paying her back from his wages. He sent postcards home from each port he visited. One still prized in the family shows his ship, *HMS Southampton*, lying at anchor in Kiel Harbour during the Kaiser's review of the German fleet just before the outbreak of war. David thought even then there was tension in the air.

The British Fleet in Kiel Harbour before the war. *HMS Southampton*, extreme right.

Miss Jenny Humphreys' collection

141

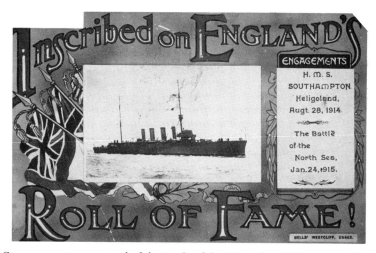

Commemorative postcard of the Battle of the North Sea, 28th August 1914.

Miss Jenny Humphreys' collection

Soon after war broke out he was involved as an Able Seaman gunner in the actions of *Southampton* off Heligoland, August 1914, and in the Dogger Bank, January 1915, receiving a prize bounty for the sinking of the *Blucher*. In that battle *Southampton* was the first British ship to open fire, and the *Blucher*, the rearguard of four heavy enemy ships, went down after three hours' heroic resistance to concentrated shelling from a number of British ships. Shortly afterwards there was great excitement aboard *Southampton* when a low-flying Zeppelin appeared. They fired at it, but without success.

David returned on leave in May 1916. All the family wanted to be seen with him, especially as he was the only one in Harlech who came home in Navy Blue, the others of course being in khaki. At the end of his leave he caught the early morning train, saying goodbye to Jenny who was still in bed. He gave her a shilling which she kept for many years but, sadly, it was eventually lost. That was the last time they saw each other.

A few days later he was involved in the thick of the action in the Battle of Jutland. *HMS Southampton* was the Flagship of the 2nd Light Cruiser Squadron, the other ships being *Nottingham, Birmingham* and *Dublin*, all 'Town' class ships, easily recognised by their four

142

funnels. *Southampton* carried the flag of Commodore Goodenough, his function and that of his squadron being to scout and report the enemy's movements. It was *Southampton* that spotted the German battleships of the High Seas Fleet in line ahead at 4.33 p.m. on 31st May, an impressive and thrilling sight that must have held the British spellbound. Throughout the rest of that momentous day Goodenough and his squadron sent consistently accurate reports back to the fleet about the movements of the enemy, each report a perfect example of first class scouting. For hours on end they were under fire but they seemed to bear a charmed life and were not hit.

After dark the squadron disengaged, but at 10.20 p.m. they suddenly and quite unexpectedly found themselves within 1,000 yards of five powerful enemy cruisers, Admiral Reuter's 4th Scout Group,

Aboard *HMS Southampton*: David Humphreys is second from the left.

Miss Jenny Humphreys' collection

143

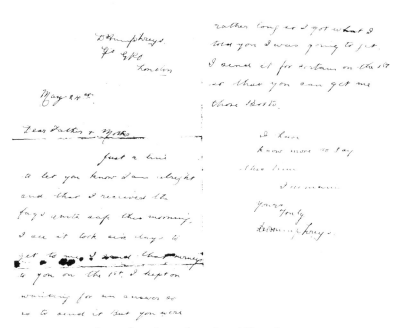

Letter from home from David Humphreys.

engaged in the same task as themselves. Immediately searchlights lit up the *Southampton* and *Dublin*, followed by salvoes of shells hitting both ships to devastating effect, the fire of four of the enemy being concentrated directly on *Southampton*. The other two ships, *Nottingham* and *Birmingham*, apparently were not at first seen, nor had they revealed their position by switching on their own searchlights. In a bitter fire fight lasting no more than four minutes and at almost point-blank range these two groups of nine ships fought each other. The German fire was deadly and the damage suffered by *Southampton* was severe. There were ten holes in her hull, there was a big fire at the rear of the funnels and numerous smaller fires elsewhere; three guns were out of action and two searchlights also.

Stephen King-Hall, later Baron King-Hall, and who was to become famous as a politician, writer and broadcaster, was a young lieutenant on board *Southampton*. In later years he wrote, 'Flesh and blood cannot stand high explosives and there was a great deal of high

144

explosive bursting along *Southampton*'s decks that night.' Many of the ship's gun crews were casualties. In all there were thirty-four dead and thirty-six wounded, a high figure. Later, in the stillness of the night when the battle was over, the bodies of the British dead were committed to the deep in that age-old naval ceremony that is so sad and yet so moving.

H.M.S. BIRMINGHAM.

Dear Mr. Humphreys –
Your son died a glorious death in defence of a glorious cause. He was buried in that most honourable place – the North Sea. I read the Burial Service over them the day after the action. Believe me you have the deep sympathy of myself & all on board.

William E. Goodenough
Commodore.

Letter from Commodore Goodenough on the death of David Humphreys.

Miss Jenny Humphreys' collection

145

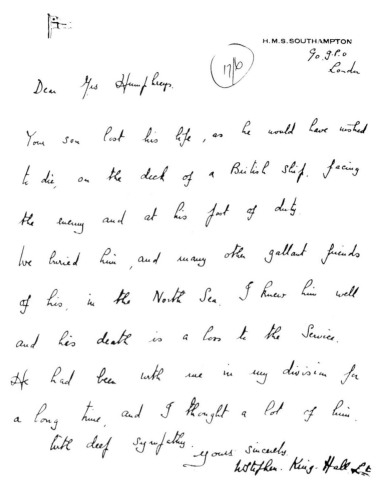

H.M.S. SOUTHAMPTON
Go.g.P.o
London

Dear Mrs Humphreys.

Your son lost his life, as he would have wished to die, on the deck of a British ship, facing the enemy and at his post of duty.

We buried him, and many other gallant friends of his, in the North Sea. I knew him well and his death is a loss to the Service. He had been with me in my division for a long time, and I thought a lot of him.

With deep sympathy. yours sincerely,
W Stephen. King-Hall Lt

Letter from Lieutenant King-Hall on the death of David Humphreys.

Miss Jenny Humphreys' collection

News of the immense naval battle filtered through to Harlech and it became the topic of general conversation on the streets of the town. Jenny remembers her mother's unease one evening as a moth flew around a flickering candle and was in due course consumed by the flame. To country people this was always a bad omen. Mrs. Humphreys looked at her husband in dismay. 'We are sure to hear some news in the morning,' he said, trying to console her. They did hear, on the morning of 3rd June, but it was bad news—the news of

David's death. Mrs. Humphreys was prostrate with grief and cried bitterly for days. 'Though I have all the others I still can't bear to lose him,' she said.

The letters received from his Divisional Officer, Lieutenant Stephen King-Hall and from Commodore Goodenough were a great comfort, and reflect great credit on these two fine officers who found time despite their own stress to write to the next-of-kin.

The years went by, but the passage of time did not heal his mother's grief, and after David's death she never again liked going down to the sea.

Jenny Humphreys, 1987.

As a young boy Ellis Owen was never well. Therefore, as soon as possible after he left school the doctor sent him to work on a farm. '*Digon o ogla anifeiliaid,* '(Plenty of animal smells) he said. So it was to the soil that Ellis went, to a farm called Morfa Mawr. He lived there many years, although not happily. The food was poor and consisted mostly, it seemed to him, of a great mass of porridge. On complaining that he couldn't chew it (*"Fedra i ddim 'i gnoi o'*), he was told not to chew it, but swallow it!

Being unable to swallow either porridge or farm any longer he ran away to Porthmadog and joined the army, the first boy from Harlech to do so before the war. But within two months of joining Ellis wanted to leave. He wrote home asking for £15 in order to buy himself out. Somehow his mother found it for him and he returned home, first to Morfa Mawr and then to Tyddyn Du farms. Here he was happy as he worked in the fields, singing in a pleasant light tenor voice all the day long. The horses kept pace as he turned the ground and even the bull, a fiercesome creature, came to know his voice and to eat out of his hand.

But wanderlust came once more and soon, in the summer of 1913, he re-joined the army, this time going to Ireland. He returned home on leave on a number of occasions, always looking the very picture of a soldier in his smart red tunic. Again, however, he grew unhappy and again wanted to buy himself out. This time his mother had to find £20 but she was able to borrow it from her brother. Once more Ellis returned home.

A few months later war broke out and so, for the third time, in August 1914, he re-joined the Colours, the Royal Welch Fusiliers, 1st/7th Battalion. Army life was in him, and yet not. He went to Wrexham, then to Rushden for training, and now, with a purpose at last to his life, he made good. Over the next nine or ten months he was promoted to Corporal and then to Sergeant.

On 4th July 1915 they received orders to prepare for service in the Dardanelles, and within ten days the battalion, with a total strength of twenty-nine officers and 969 other ranks, had left Devonport on three separate ships. They arrived in Egypt on 28th July, joining the

Expeditionary Force on 1st August. They left Port Said for the Dardanelles at 7 o'clock on the morning of 4th August and, in an almost leisurely voyage across the eastern Mediterranean, they reached Mudros at noon three days later. They left there in light draught small boats the following day in mounting excitement, their instructions being to leave everything behind that could not be carried. They reached their landing point, Suvla Bay, on the evening of 8th August.

They lay offshore for most of the night, beginning their disembarkation at first light. By 7 a.m. they were all ashore. There was heavy Turkish shelling on the beaches, so they were quickly moved a mile or so inland amid a terrain of flat scrub and stunted trees to the west of a small hill called Lala Baba. Here they bivouacked until the morning of 10th August. At 4.30 a.m. the whole Brigade, the 158th, consisting of the 5th, 6th, 1st/7th Royal Welch Fusiliers and the 2nd/10th Middlesex, was ordered to relieve 159th Brigade and to advance a mile beyond the point of contact, towards Sulajik. Unfortunately, it wasn't known that 159th Brigade had already been withdrawn, so the 158th came under unexpectedly heavy rifle and shrapnel fire. As the day wore on they tried to struggle forward but the Turks increased the intensity of their resistance and counter-attacked fiercely. There was confusion everywhere. For a long time the battalion was pinned down and there were extremely heavy casualties, amongst them, tragically, Ellis, who was killed sometime during the early afternoon. There, at Suvla Bay, so many miles away from home, he was the first Harlech boy to be killed in the war.

The news of his death came through on a lovely summer's day in the town, with a warm sun beating down from a cloudless sky. It somehow made the news more difficult to bear, and his mother wept and wept, with her husband trying desperately to console her in any way he could.

Accounts of the manner of his death gradually filtered back as members of his battalion in due course returned home on leave. They all spoke of his popularity, and of the thorough and efficient way he had trained his section. On this day, pinned down as they were by the deadly accurate Turkish rifle fire, he had shouted at them, *'Eich pennau i lawr i gyd. Dim un i godi ei ben'* (Heads down, all of you. No one to raise his head). Unfortunately, he did not follow his own instructions and as he inched his head up to try and observe the enemy's movements he was shot and died instantly with a bullet through the temple.

Turkish shelling was now so intense that the whole brigade was forced to retreat and, in the chaos that followed, Ellis's body, sadly, was never recovered. He has no known grave, but his name is commemorated on the beautiful Helles memorial at Gallipoli. He was twenty-five years old.

ROBERT LEWIS OWEN

Ellis's brother, Bob, even as a child, was a great organiser. One of the best organised 'funerals' ever held in Harlech was to bury Tom, the cat. And Bob took charge. Old Tom had given all the outward signs of death. Consequently Bob got together ten or so 'mourners' to walk in procession down to a pond known by the grisly name of *'Llyn boddi cathod'* (The lake to drown cats). Bob himself carried the sack with the body of old Tom in it. At the poolside there was simulated crying, a short service of 'prayer' and then the sack was flung hard and high into the air, to land with a splash right in the middle. They all watched the 'spot' in some sort of fascinated horror. Then the water was seen to churn and move. With terrified screams from the girls rending the air, they all turned as one and fled, with a bedraggled and not-so-dead cat swimming for all his worth towards the shore. He arrived home later, wet and miserable, but really none the worse, and obtained a well-deserved reprieve.

When Bob Owen grew up he wanted to start his own business as a cobbler. He had started as an apprentice straight from school and eventually his mother proudly went to Porthmadog to buy him the kit that he would need to start up on his own. Eventually he opened a small shop in Llanbedr, a few miles from Harlech, developing a good business and working there for two or three years.

Unlike his brother the army never attracted Bob, even when war broke out. But he did want to play his part. So, without ostentation, early in 1915 he went to South Wales to join up, being recruited into the 12th Battalion King's Royal Rifle Corps.

His mother fretted terribly, especially in the first weeks after the loss of Ellis. Her faith had weakened considerably and she had not been to chapel since his death. However, as time went on, and Robert kept safe, she became calmer. Her husband, whose own beliefs had never faltered, but who never reproached his wife, just kept hoping that her faith would return. And then, on a lovely Monday morning in October (1915) she said she would come to chapel that day for *Diolch-garwch* (Thanksgiving), such services traditionally being held on Mondays. Mr. Owen broke down. *'Diolch i Dduw'* (Thanks to God), he whispered.

The day was so warm that the windows were wide open and the curtains were fluttering in the breeze. It was a day very similar to that on which they had learned of the death of Ellis. Mr. Owen was in the garden while his wife was dressing. Olwen, their daughter, was ready, waiting downstairs. Mrs. Owen called down to say that she could see the postman coming with three or four letters. She came down the stairs as the letters clattered to the floor and she asked Olwen to open them. On the top was a Field Card from Bob. It said: 'I am well. Robert Owen.'

Olwen then opened a long, brown, official envelope. She read the words, but could hardly believe what she was reading. It was a War Office letter informing them that Bob had been killed in action. She was numb with horror. Her mother by now was reading the card as Mr. Owen came in.

'Letter, Gwen?'

'There's a card from Bob,' she said.

'Good—nice to know he's alive and well. What have you got, Olwen?'

Olwen didn't know what to do, what to say or how to say it. She was only fourteen. She said simply, *'Mae Bob wedi'i ladd'* (Bob's been killed). They all stood still, stunned.

A neighbour, Catrin Roberts, came in. She saw that they were upset. She read the letter, silently made them a cup of tea and left, shutting the door on their private grief. But bad news travels fast. All Harlech knew of Bob's death before the start of the morning Thanksgiving service. 'We didn't go,' says Olwen.

151

The months passed. Olwen and her father continued attending chapel but without Mrs. Owen. Eventually Mr. Owen asked his wife to come with them: *'Mae'r sêt yn wag. Dowch efo ni eto'* (The seat is empty. Come with us again). *'Ga'i weld'* (I'll see), she replied.

A few Saturdays after that conversation Mrs. Owen was preparing supper with Olwen's help. Suddenly she put the cutlery down and said that she would come to chapel the following day. *'Awn ni, ein tri bach'* (We'll go, we three). Mr. Owen was home from a long week's work at the quarry and was washing his hands at the outside tap. Olwen found an excuse to go out and whisper, *'Dad, mae Mam yn dod i'r capel'* (Dad, Mum's coming to chapel). Her father said nothing, but his eyes filled with tears. 'She came, and it pleased us all,' says Olwen, 'Mam, too, though I doubt if it lightened the sadness of losing two fine boys.'

Robert lies buried in Plot 2, Row A at No. 1 Military Cemetery, near Laventie, on the road between St. Omer and Armentieres, 1,200 miles away from where his brother was killed two months earlier.

GRIFFITH M. THOMAS

Griff Thomas was born in February 1900 in the old Baptist chapel by then converted into a shop. His father, unable to make a living there as a butcher, moved the family to Blaenau Ffestiniog in 1902. There he obtained work in the Oakley quarry, not on the rock face but in the machine shed. This suited him, for he had lost a leg in an accident in that quarry in the early 1890s. However, the family returned to Harlech in May 1914, although Mr. Thomas continued to work for three days a week in Blaenau. Despite an artificial leg he walked the six miles to Penrhyn early on Mondays to catch the quarrymen's train (the famous Ffestiniog Railway), returning the same way each Wednesday evening.

For a few months after leaving school Griff worked mornings for twelve shillings a week, a good sum in those days, cleaning shoes and brasses in one of the bigger houses in Harlech, Bron Heulog. In the afternoons he went caddying on the golf course at ninepence a round, with a tip of about threepence.

By November 1914 William Owen the butcher wanted a carrying-out boy to replace Griffith Lloyd who had joined the army, and who was eventually killed at Gaza in March 1917. As they lived opposite the butcher, Griff jumped at the chance of working for Mr. Owen, one of the advantages being that the pony and cart could be used to take his father down to Penrhyn to catch his train. By 1915, however, Mr. Thomas had rejoined his family in Harlech, finding employment at the St. David's Hotel garage.

In the meantime Griff tried his hand at farming, going to Cae Du at a rate of £6 per half year. He knew nothing about farming and he found it heavy going, especially the task of picking up hundreds of small stones to prevent the blunting of scythes or mower, and placing them on the dry stone walls. ('I swear the stones grew nightly in those fields!') In 1917 he became a general help to a builder in Cricieth, but in the meantime his father had become seriously ill and Griff returned to Harlech. His father died of cancer in the September.

'My father had been friendly with the famous poet, Hedd Wyn, who had visited our home in Blaenau one Saturday to discuss poetry. He was killed in Flanders and father was given the sad news not long before he himself died.' (Hedd Wyn, known as the 'Shepherd Poet', had just won the Bardic Chair at the National Eisteddfod in August 1917, but his death on Pilkem Ridge on 31st July left the coveted prize unclaimed. In a moving and dramatic ceremony the empty chair was left on stage, draped starkly in black.)

After his father's death, Griff found work as a labourer in an open cast manganese mine on the Rhinog hills behind Harlech, the mine eventually giving work to about twelve people in all. Their main task was to extract the manganese and carry it in barrows to the tip nearby for it to be taken downhill by horse and cart.

By 1918 it was time for Griff to join up. His employer wanted to get him released from call-up on the grounds that he was doing work of national importance. Griff's mother, naturally, agreed but he himself wanted to go because all the other lads had already gone or were about to. 'I did have a few weeks before I joined the Army, which pleased me, for though I wanted to go away and see the world I wasn't in all that much of a hurry to see the next!'

Griff Thomas before leaving for Germany, Herne Bay, 1918. He was then in 4th
Battalion Royal Welch Fusiliers.

He went to Wrexham, joining the Royal Welch Fusiliers. Eventually he was posted to Herne Bay where he was transferred to the South Wales Borderers, the 24th Regiment of Foot. 'As they were the 24th they put their puttees on in a particular way, in a pattern of two crosses (to represent two tens) and four single leg encirclements, making twenty-four in all. Very confusing for a raw recruit!'

One day he and his friends were put on punishment by the Corporal because he said someone had sworn at him at breakfast that morning, although Griff denied it. That evening they were forced to do one hour's pack drill, marching and counter-marching. The injustice of it rankled and Griff was determined to get his own back. 'I intended to teach this particular NCO a lesson he wouldn't forget in a hurry and I told my friends what I proposed to do during the next poison gas drill. My gas mask was thought to be suspect because it was slightly loose, though I myself knew it was all right. We got inside the gas hut, all with our masks on, with the Corporal, as usual, coming in with us. Knowing that he was watching and with the gas gradually filling the hut I pretended to be overcome by the fumes, closing my eyes, staggering a little and dropping my head down to my chest. By the time he screamed for me to be pulled out he was sweating profusely. "I thought you were dying," he said. I just looked at him and smiled.'

From Herne Bay they moved to Ipswich and from there to the outskirts of Bury St. Edmunds. Orders then came for the move to France, but before they went Armistice was declared. By the time they arrived in Dunkirk the war was well and truly over. Orders then came for entrainment for Germany, a goods train, with straw as bedding. It was a terrible journey, cold and miserable, and for four days they suffered until their arrival at Munstereifel. Here they were to form part of the post-war army of occupation.

On their first night in Germany, while looking for a billet, three or four of them found temporary sleeping accommodation in an attic. On the way upstairs one evil-looking German stared at them menacingly and, it seemed to Griff, at him in particular. It scared him out of his wits. He was feverish also, with a touch of flu. He slept nearest the attic door, nervously, his bayonet at his side. 'He'll get you first, Taff!' someone teased. In the middle of the night the door opened slowly and Griff, waking in panic, threw the bayonet at it.

Horselines, 75 Company Royal Engineers, Munstereifel, Germany, 1918. Griff
Thomas is standing by the wall.

G. Thomas' collection

'What's that?' asked one of the others as the clatter woke him but
Griff, too, was now wide awake and realised that he had been
dreaming.

'It was my rifle falling over,' he said lamely.

'Well leave the bloody thing alone and get back to sleep.'

'Although the war was over there was still a feeling of enmity
towards us,' says Griff, 'and during my first week in Munstereifel I
felt this very strongly. One day I was walking down the street when I
saw some of our boys being given a shave and haircut. Thinking it was
an approved barber's shop I entered. But the barber seemed to me to
be just as evil-looking a German as the other, and he was big and thickset as well. I began to feel uneasy. As the shop emptied I found that I
was the last customer, and when I sat down in his chair he drew the
blinds and locked the door. As he lathered my face I broke into a lather
also, and as that razor was gently stroked over my throat I thought my
last moments had come. I breathed a great sigh of relief when I eventually got out into the street!'

Food in the camp was sparse and poor because their rations had not
reached them, but by great good fortune he met Griffith Humphreys
(brother of David who was killed at Jutland), and whom he had last

156

seen and talked to when they were both on leave in Harlech. Griffith told him they had spare rations in their billet and, taking Griff there, loaded him with bread, butter and a tin of jam which he later shared with his own appreciative billet.

Griff, wanting to work with animals, now applied for a transfer to the Veterinary Corps. He did not succeed in that but was posted to the Royal Engineers. One of the first mules he had to tend and take to the trough was extremely vicious, the worst he'd ever known. It jumped and kicked and bit. Later, when he asked the Corporal the name of this frightening beast, the Corporal replied, 'Jesus.'

'Why do you call him that?'

'Because that's what they all say when they get hold of him!'

Shortly before leaving Germany his unit was inspected by General Sir William Robertson who had left the appointment of Chief of the Imperial General Staff and was now Commander-in-Chief of the British Army of Occupation. He stopped in front of Griff and in that

Royal Engineers' stable piquet somewhere in Germany, 1919. Griff Thomas on the left.

G. Thomas' collection

157

Griff Thomas, 1987.

famous Lincolnshire accent asked him where he came from. 'From Harlech, Sir,' said Griff proudly. The great man was about to move on when he glanced back at Griff and said, 'Well done, young man, for keeping up the tradition.'

Griff eventually returned to the United Kingdom in August 1919 and obtained a weekend pass to Harlech. He got the last train from London to Porthmadog and from there, a distance of ten miles, he walked home, whistling and singing all the way, arriving at about two o'clock in the morning. He banged on the door. His brother Johnny leaned out of an upstairs window. Who was there at that time of night? '*Agor y drws*,' Griff shouted, '*i mi gael mynd i 'ngwely*' (Open the door, so I can get to my bed).

He was eventually demobilised in November 1919. On his last day in Aldershot he remembers King George V visiting army units there, accompanied by the Shah of Persia, but Griff himself was more excited at the prospect of going home. And so, seventy years on, after working once more as a labourer in Rhinog manganese mine, as a coal miner for six months in South Wales, as a journeyman craftsman in the building industry, as a railway porter and as an insurance agent during the Second World War, he now lives with his wife Peggy in contented retirement in the town where he was born, still retaining that witty and gentle humour he had as a young man.

JOHNNY WILLIAMS

Johnny Williams was born in Harlech in 1898, the fourth in a family of eight sisters and two brothers, and still lives in the town, still known affectionately as 'Johnny Postman' after nearly a lifetime spent in post office work. His father worked in the quarries of Blaenau Ffestiniog. There, in dismal conditions, he lodged for 1/- per week, sleeping in barrack accommodation, in a bed shared between two or three, returning on the two o'clock train each Saturday still grimy with slate dust. Johnny left school at fourteen but did not follow in his father's footsteps. Somewhat fortuitously, he got a job as a telegraph boy, the vacancy occurring when his friend Morris John, who worked in the Post Office, suddenly ran away to sea. Johnny and Morris were playing together on the golf course one day and the next day Morris had gone. Being unable to find the fare to Liverpool he found a ship that would take him in Porthmadog. 'So I took his job,' said Johnny. 'He was at sea for the rest of his life and I was in the post office for the rest of mine.'

Although he was a telegraph boy he also delivered parcels, and occasionally letters if the postman was ill. He was paid piece-rate, for each telegram and each letter, twopence at first, then threepence. He used to sit on the wall waiting for instructions, with bike alongside. 'You paid for your own bike, replacement tyres and all.' The bike was all-important. You *could* get a post office job without one, but it would be difficult, for delivering telegrams to the hill farms would be virtually impossible. Johnny recalls going up to Cwm Bychan farm with a telegram, six miles up into the hills, only to find on returning to the Post Office that he had to go all the way back with another. But he wasn't busy all the time, and he sometimes played billiards as he waited, or sat talking in the cobbler's shop or mended punctures. When a telegram came he delivered it and put the item down in his log book. The postmaster then gave him his money at the end of the week.

Soldiers outside the Harlech Post Office.

Author's collection

160

However, he was not established yet. That took time. 'You had to be a certain age before you became established, and to be an established telegraph boy you had to work in Head Office; Harlech was only a sub-Post Office also selling ladies' wear, groceries, paraffin and general goods.'

At Harlech, the mail was brought up the hill from the station two or three times a day. The staff used the trolley in the mornings but in the evenings they usually carried the mail themselves, in sacks. All four members of staff, plus one extra for the summer holidays, wore their own clothes, with a red GPO badge on the left arm, and they always had straw hats for the summer.

Johnny's patch included the coast road to Llanfair and the whole of Llandanwg parish, three or four miles each way. There was a pig dealer in Llanfair, David Williams, who received two telegrams a week, Mondays and Thursdays, with the latest pig prices in Birmingham. At sixpence a journey this was worth a shilling a week, valuable and regular income. There was also extra cash for longer journeys—a shilling to Cwm Bychan, for example. For parcels there was a permanent wage—three shillings a week. Johnny delivered parcels all around the town, to the golf club, Plas Amherst, St. David's Hotel and Wern Fawr. For this purpose he had a hand truck with a large basket. 'I used to pull it like a mule.' There was also a small trolley with two wheels. 'You pulled it up hill and you pushed it down—if you were foolish enough!' The baskets could be left anywhere and there was never a theft, although the big basket did have a lid which could be fastened and locked. But the only time the lid was on was when it was raining.

One of the post office characters was Dick 'Talar Tina' (the name of the terrace where he lived). Dick, a man with a wobbly moustache and always with plenty to say, never worked with his hat on. The postmaster at that time, Mr. Griffiths, always tried to work within post office regulations (hats and ties, no smoking on duty) and he succeeded with everyone except Dick. One morning Dick came into the Post Office, as usual without his hat. Mr. Griffiths asked him where it was. '*Dyma fo,*' said Dick. '*Gwisgwch hi'ch hun, y diawl*' (Here it is, wear the bloody thing yourself) and with that he flung it on

161

Johnny Williams, before embarking for France.

the counter, marched out of the Post Office and never came back. He got himself a job as a car driver for old Dr. Jones.

'One of our regular visits,' says Johnny, 'was to the house of Mari Thomas. She sold shoes and therefore received numerous parcels. But she often stayed in bed until midday and, not wanting us to leave parcels outside, would leave the bedroom window open. I'd have to climb the drainpipe, pass through her bedroom, saying "Good morning" as I went and then go downstairs to unlock the front door— in order to let the cats out as well as deliver parcels!'

A regular task twice a week, on Tuesdays and Fridays, was to collect from the station the fish that was sent from Grimsby, and then to deliver it as quickly as possible to the larger houses and to the St. David's Hotel. There was a fish and vegetable shop in Harlech run by Will Roberts and it was always a source of irritation to him that these establishments did not buy from his shop. One day one of these 'big pots', as Roberts called them, old Colonel Lloyd, was walking past his shop and noticed Will's car outside.

'Humph. Your car then, Will?'

'Yes,' said Will, arms languidly folded, leaning back against the door. 'But I couldn't even buy a wheelbarrow with the help you give me.'

'Ah, you see, Will, I grow enough vegetables in my own garden, don't I?'

'Yes, but you don't grow fish, do you?'

Johnny eventually joined the Royal Welch Fusiliers in 1916. He had his medical at Wrexham and his training took place at Kinmel Park, Rhyl. He did not remain with the Regiment long, for he was transferred to the 8th (City of London) Post Office Rifles. There were no other Welshmen in the battalion, which he thought a pity. He joined them in Torquay, going to France early in 1917. The Post Office Rifles had been badly mauled in action at St. Quentin, with over fifty per cent casualties, and on his arrival in France he was transferred yet again, this time to the Rifle Brigade who were involved in bitter fighting on the Somme. For many long, miserable months he was in the trenches.

Then came the immense German offensive of Spring 1918, the breakthrough and the Allied retreat. 'It was far worse retreating than

Johnny Williams in postman's uniform, after the war.

J. Williams' collection.

attacking. At least if you were attacking you knew what to expect.' All was chaos. He found himself manning a Lewis gun amongst French troops with German field grey infiltrating to the right. There was a tremendous cacophony of sound from a troop of French artillery nearby, and Johnny thinks his hearing (he is partly deaf) was affected by that particular bombardment. He also met the first of the American Expeditionary Force. 'Where are those krauts?' one of them asked. 'You'll find them,' said Johnny.

The battalion eventually found itself in a fairly quiet town near Villers Bretton, although the Germans were never far away. A cellar full of wine had been found and volunteers were asked to take some to the front line. 'I was never a heavy drinker,' says Johnny, 'but I used to quite like the rum, and knowing that a bottle of wine would be a welcome addition to the rations, I volunteered.' So, laden with bottles, watching for machine-gun fire, he moved up to the front line. Suddenly there was a loud explosion overhead, and the next thing he remembers on waking is looking at his shattered left leg, with a gaping shrapnel wound in the upper thigh.

His memory is fitful after that. He recalls being in a cellar, moving by ambulance to Amiens, gunfire overhead. He was many months in hospital, in France and England. Finally, on the morning of Armistice Day he was moved to the military hospital in Salisbury. There they wanted to amputate his leg, but his family forbade it. He was moved from Salisbury to Sutton Coldfield, eventually returning home to Harlech in 1919. 'And as for the leg—I have it still.'*

When Johnny first joined the army as an unestablished post boy he could not be certain that he would get his old job back: 'Though if you were liked well enough they would try their best on your behalf.' Whilst he was away his job had been done by a woman, Mary Elin, but she left soon after the war ended and, although at first he wasn't keen, his family persuaded him to take the vacancy.

Originally, the delivery of letters to far-away farms had been once every two days. Now, partly because of an increase in postal volume

*Unfortunately the leg eventually *was* amputated, but not until 1988. It is good to report that Johnny has recovered well and is in good health.

but also in order to create work for returning ex-servicemen, delivery was increased to once daily. Although his damaged leg meant that he had to push his bike up steep hill tracks he could still coast downwards. He received a warm welcome everywhere but it was hard work, especially in cold weather. There was still no uniform, a cape only ('And that was rubbish') so his clothes got worn and wet.

Johnny also increased some part-time work he was doing for old Dr. Jones in the afternoons, at the same time teaching himself to drive. The doctor's son, Orthin, ex-RAMC, in due course took over his father's practice, and Johnny drove for him. He felt he was useful to the young doctor because he knew the people and knew the roads. But cars in those days were perverse creatures. They often stalled on the steep hills and had to be reversed down-hill in order to get up enough speed to take the hill at full pelt. 'Often, too, when petrol was low we had to go backwards up slopes in order to create a flow of petrol down to the engine from the tank under the back seat, there being no pump for the petrol in those early days.'

Johnny continues: 'Dr. Orthin Jones was an excellent doctor and a fine man. It was he who gave me the first contribution to the British Legion for a Harlech ex-serviceman, Evan Pugh, who had been blinded. Dr. Jones's wife, also a lovely person, came from a wealthy Caernarfon family who had lived many years in Egypt. In the war years they'd held open house in their Cairo home for Welsh boys stationed in the Near East.'

Eventually, in 1924, a full-time appointment became vacant in the post office at £2.10s.0d. per week. Johnny took it, remaining there for forty three years until his eventual retirement in 1967. For many years, too, he led an active life in the British Legion and he still maintains a controlling interest as the owner of the Harlech Caravan site. He is known and respected by English and overseas visitors as much as by local people.

'The aristocracy no longer come to Harlech as they used to, and for weeks on end,' he says. 'But visitors do come, more and more each year. That's good, because Harlech is still a beautiful place.'

Is there anything that is poorer? 'Yes, the Post Office is poorer. There are vans everywhere, of course, but the mail delivery is less reliable. And the collections seem illogical; letters must now go to

Porthmadog, ten miles away, before delivery to Llanfair, two miles away. And it's the Porthmadog stamp that's on the envelope. In the old days people all over the world got envelopes stamped in Harlech. They got to know about Harlech that way. Not now, and it's sad, very sad.'